4361

LIFE IS A ZOO—
NO MATTER WHAT SIDE OF THE CAGE YOU'RE ON

Life Is a Zoo—

No Matter What Side of the Cage You're on

Gary Richmond

VB
VINE
BOOKS

Servant Publications
Ann Arbor, Michigan

Vine Books is an imprint of Servant Publications
especially designed to serve Evangelical Christians.

Published by Servant Publications
P.O. Box 8617
Ann Arbor, Michigan 48107

Cover design by Michael Andaloro
Cover photo by Tim Stahl, San Diego, California

A special thanks to the finest zoo in the world, the San Diego Zoo,
for their help in setting up the cover photograph and to
Georgeanne Irvine, Director of Public Relations

92 93 94 95 96 10 9 8 7 6 5 4

Printed in the United States of America

ISBN 0-89283-760-8

Library of Congress Cataloging-in-Publication Data

Richmond, Gary.
    Life is a zoo— / no matter what side of the cage you're on /
Gary Richmond.
        p. cm.
    ISBN 0-89283-760-8
    1. Richmond, Gary, 1944—Childhood and youth. 2. United
States—Biography. I. Title.
    CT275.R5592A3   1992
    973.92'092—dc20   92-1154

Dedication

Anything of an autobiographical nature should be dedicated to those who have had to endure life with the main character. These people would of course be relatives. So it is with apologies, love, and thanksgiving that I dedicate Life Is a Zoo to...

My cherished wife Carol (Boy, could she bury me.)
My oldest daughter Marci (She introduced us to raising children.)
My youngest daughter Wendi (She just got married.)
My son Gary who is sixteen (Pray for us.)
Marci's husband Joe and Wendi's husband Tommy (My two favorite sons-in-law.)
Life is still a zoo, but it's okay—I love zoos.

Contents

Introduction

I HAVE BEEN TOLD that there are just two kinds of people: those that let things happen and those that make things happen. For whatever reason I have always been the latter. Because of this I have very few empty yesterdays and buckets full of fun stories to share with anyone with a moment or two to sit and take them in.

In this book, I have woven together numerous stories from my life to make for you a tapestry of hope. You see, I was raised in what has come to be called a dysfunctional family. In our family I was surrounded by alcoholics, unaddressed problems and great excesses. My alcoholic mother was severely depressed and suicidal. My father was a recovered alcoholic, and a recovered gambler, and I remember him as a hardworking provider, faithful husband, and a wonderful dad for as long as my brother and I had him. He died when I was fifteen and life should have fallen apart then but it didn't.

Given my early years I should be in jail now but I am not. I am happily married. I am the proud father of three children, two lovely girls who are teachers and happily married and a sixteen year old boy who is an honors student. I am currently working at the First Evangelical Free Church of Fullerton California as the pastor for a group of eight hundred single parents and their children. I have lots of close friends and wouldn't trade lives with anyone you or I know. I am, in short, a satisfied customer of God's amazing grace.

I wrote this book to make you laugh and to bring you hope. If your story is anything like mine, you might be wondering how it's all going to turn out. Like me, you are writing a story with your life. You may be in a dark and dreary chapter but keep turning those pages. The better days are just ahead so wait for them and they'll come maybe just in time. Let me cheer you with some of the best stories of my life. Let me prove that life is a zoo no matter what side of the cage you're on.

1

In Pursuit of Manhood

THE MALE IDENTITY CRISIS skipped my generation. We knew being a man meant being like John Wayne. He was rough-shod but clever, a two-fisted, independent, opinionated, hard-drinking, fearless man of his word. Animals loved him, women adored him, and men were silent in his presence. Quiet until riled, "the Duke" was kind to the down-trodden but trouble to evildoers.

John Wayne was somehow above even the small frailties of the common man. When others got drunk, they looked stupid. But not the Duke, who seemed to know just the right time to get drunk. If he acted a little silly, his manhood appeared even more adorable. Most men looked a bit vulgar when they spit; John Wayne just looked more like a man. Real men spit when they want to. Even better, they hit what they aim for!

Our family was the first on the block to own a television, so I was raised on John Wayne westerns and war classics. He never backed down from a fight and always seemed to triumph in the face of overwhelming odds. I watched him rush into battle, die for a grand cause, and go down with his ship. He was something.

There has never been a man quite like John Wayne, nor is there likely to be. The Duke was simply the standard-bearer of manhood—justice, bravery, patriotism, strength, and honor rolled into one. I later watched him grow old and die a little ahead of his time because of too many drinks and too many cigarettes. But in the eyes of a boy, he seemed above the weaknesses that plagued the common man. John Wayne was my banner, my standard, the drummer to which I marched to manhood. To be like him would be to have achieved the quest, climbed the mountain, finished the journey.

MY QUEST BEGUN

I remember the day I began my quest to become a man. My closest friend managed to pick a fight with an eighth grader who seemed twice his size. I can't recall what provoked the fight, but I think the other guy had put my friend down for being short. Ronald was one of the shortest guys in our seventh grade class, but he was perky and full of pluck.

Fighting was the rule of conduct at Elliot Junior High School in Altadena, California. The drama proceeded along very predictable lines. The combatants walked one-half block to the back parking lot of the Market Basket and waited for a crowd to gather. They stood face-to-face and called each other names for a minute or two. Then one would say, "Did you come here to talk or fight?" The other would say, "I'm here, what are you waiting for?" After the first guy repeated the same question, someone in the crowd would say, "Are you guys chicken or what?"

That usually did it. The two who came to fight would start pushing each other and one would say, "Come on, let's do it." Then the other would say, "What are you waiting for?" Tempers would flare and finally the fight would begin. Part of the ritual was spreading the word about the scheduled fight. Consequently, the vice-principal almost always showed up to break it up before anything got started. Maybe some never really wanted to fight and hoped he would come in time.

The vice-principal didn't come that day, but fifty kids came expecting to see a bloodbath. Ronny and Bill stood in the middle of the circle. The ritual proceeded according to the script for several minutes without any blows being thrown. Ronny was clearly the underdog and everyone was hoping to see him clean Bill's plow, but that mainly happens in the movies.

When the fight finally started Bill kicked the stuffing out of Ronny in short order, but my friend had too much pride to give up. The crowd was enjoying the gory spectacle. I wasn't. Ronny's mouth and nose were bleeding and his shirt was torn. Bill didn't have a scratch on him. Ronny took another blow to the face and fell down. With tears in his eyes, he started to get up for more.

I couldn't handle anymore. I stepped in front of Ronny and looked Bill in the eye and said, "Why don't you pick on someone your own size?" Bill was basking in his one-sided victory and sneered, "You're pretty close to my size." I stared at him with hatred and spat back, "That's the way I see it." Ronny seemed a little miffed that I had upstaged him and tried to push me out of the way, but I wouldn't let him.

I turned to Bill and he started the ritual. "Well are you just..." That's when I made my move. Quick as a flash I cracked his nose and knocked him flat. Bill bounced back up and we really got into it. It never occurred to me that I could lose, and I didn't. After taking three or four more blows to the face, Bill held up his hand and said, "I've had enough."

Happy to quit while I was ahead, I said, "Then get out of here." Ronny had cooled off and thanked me for what I had done. I told him that's what friends are for, but next time to pick a fight with someone more his size, so I wouldn't have to bail him out—or else sooner or later I would get the stuffings knocked out of me.

As far as I was concerned, I had taken my first giant step toward manhood at the age of twelve. For one spring afternoon I had been John Wayne in a good-versus-evil confrontation and had emerged victorious. I wanted to tell my dad the good news, but I was afraid he would tell my mom. Then I would get the standard "you don't have to fight to be a man" lecture that I had heard twice the year before.

I slept well that night and enjoyed the praise that came with dumping on an eighth grader. But the good feelings didn't last. Even as a seventh grader, I knew I had not established my manhood. My virility was subject to my winning, and there would always be someone I couldn't beat.

STANDING UP TO FEAR

So what did define manhood? I came to accept *fearlessness* as the essence of John Wayne's manliness. Over the next several years I periodically tried to pass from childhood to manhood under my modified definition. In high school I drove cars much too fast and risked my life and that of others in the process. But I would always become proficient at handling one level of risk and then have to kick it up a notch to prove something more. The point never came when I could confidently say, "I'm a real man."

I received Christ into my life at the age of fifteen. But since no one told me what it meant to be a man, I kept my John Wayne mentality of fearlessness as the standard.

On a camping trip at twenty-one, my close friend and comrade in adventure, Sonny Salsbury, challenged me to a contest of sorts. A high cliff overhung a crystal blue lake near our campsite. Ledges offered opportunities to jump from twenty, forty, or sixty feet into the cool, deep water.

Looking up at those heights didn't seem that big a deal so I accepted Sonny's "I will if you will" offer to jump. We climbed up part of the way and then pulled ourselves hand over hand up by the rope. After jumping from the twenty-foot ledge several times, we bravely climbed to the forty-foot level. We inched our way out to the ledge and then threw the rope back to others waiting to ascend.

I was shocked when I looked down. The pool was at least fifty feet in diameter, but from forty feet up I suddenly questioned whether I might hit the shore if I jumped with too much enthusiasm. It seemed a strong wind could even blow me into the trees. I was immediately sorry that I had made any deal involving a jump from forty feet. My only hope was that Sonny would also recognize the catastrophic possibilities and offer to call the whole thing off himself.

My hopes were dashed when my friend yelled, "Here goes!" and leapt out into space. Sonny fell quickly and disappeared into the gorgeous blue water. He made an enormous splash and was hidden by foam for several seconds. I began to think he was hurt until he reappeared and yelled, "Yahoo!" Sonny looked up at me and cried, "You'll love it! It was great! Go for it, Gare!"

"Sonny, this is higher than I thought. I'm *not* going to enjoy it, I promise." I was hoping he would let me off the hook because of the note of desperation in my voice. No such luck. He called back, "You'll have to jump. We made a deal and nobody is going to throw you the rope to get back. You'll either jump or be there for the rest of your life."

Sonny's sadistic grin made him look a bit like Jack Nicholson. The presence of high school students persuaded me not to grovel. I thought a fetal position would be convincing except that the ledge was too narrow. The forty feet now looked like a mile, but I knew Sonny and I knew there was only one way down. I just wanted to get it over with so I clinched my teeth and decided to go on the count of three.

With all the determination I could muster, I rocked back and forth and counted, "One, two, three...." I'm not sure what went wrong but I was still on the ledge—still rocking but not jumping.

Sonny's obvious pleasure over my plight provided just enough "I'll-show-you" incentive. I stood erect and began again. "One, two, THREE..., four, five, six... Oh, shoot!"

I just couldn't do it. What was I afraid of? I quickly answered my stupid question: death, pain, a forty-foot belly flop (WAAAA!), falling and drowning at the bottom of a pool.

"Sonny, get me that rope!"

"No, nope, nyet, unhuh, not now, not later, never! We made a deal. I did it, now you do it!"

This was the last deal I would ever make of this kind, I resolved. "One, two, three, four.... Oh, brother!"

My humiliation was intensified by the high school sophomore diving from the ledge twenty feet above me every ten minutes—even doing flips! Every time he passed my level on the way up he would cheerfully encourage me, "Hey, you can do it, big fella." Little show-off. What else would you expect from a sophomore? The dictionary defines sophomoric as "the feeling someone has arrived." He thought he was hot stuff doing flips from sixty feet. He made diving look so easy and me look so bad.

I stood on that ledge for two hours. My bare feet were sore and my legs were wobbly. You're probably wondering if I ever jumped. Well, I finally did. Want to know what made me do it? The time had come to return to the camp. Sonny and all the high schoolers had gathered their belongings and were just standing on the shore looking up. Tired and hungry, they could not understand my reluctance. The tone was no longer encouraging but more like come on, Gary, we want to go now. NOW!

I looked down and blurted, "One, two, THREE!" Then I leaned and my momentum carried me to the point of no leaning back even if I wanted to. I was committed. I was falling. I could feel the acceleration. It was incredible. I could feel the adrenaline squirt. My heart was pounding so ferociously I thought it would jump out of my chest. The water was rushing up at me at a threatening speed. Then suddenly I was plunging to a depth of fourteen feet in the cool water. My feet hit the bottom of the pool and pushed off to return to the surface. When my head broke through the water the small crowd was cheering wildly.

Just for a moment I was a real man again. I wondered if the Duke would have done this? Then I remembered that he had jumped off cliffs on horses lots of times from even greater heights. Oh, bother. Was I ever to become a REAL man? Maybe not.

FACING WILD ANIMALS

At twenty-three I began my career at the Los Angeles Zoo—still in search of manhood. Something told me I was going to find it there. With a thousand dangers to confront, facing one of them would surely provide the rite of passage to transform an old boy into a man. I didn't want to be Peter

Pan and never grow up, but I still didn't know how to make the transition.

Because of my quick reflexes, I soon became adept at animal capture. I remember the first time I was invited to participate in one of these dangerous ventures. To give distemper shots to coyotes, we first needed to capture them in what looked like a giant butterfly net. The heavy net was constructed of steel tubing attached to a hoop. The hoop was two feet in diameter and covered with a rubber hose to prevent injury to the animals.

Two of us went into the cage with five coyotes, one of which was known to be very vicious. I just didn't know which one! When a very capable keeper had tried to net this wily male just a few days earlier, the coyote had jumped up a wall and leapt right into the man's face. The deep bite required dozens of stitches and left a permanent facial scar. Netting coyotes was no parlor game, but that day it went without incident. I had the knack and I had the nerve. The zoo was going to be fun.

Animal capture became one of my main responsibilities when I was transferred to the zoo's health center. My job was to restrain sick or injured animals while the veterinarian examined them. Day after day I had to put my hands and body on the line for the sake of the vet and the animals. Working with other good men kept my injuries minimal for the first three years, though I did have some first-rate close calls.

One day I served above and beyond the call of duty. Jeannie, our largest and meanest female chimp, managed to break the weld on a section of the chain-link fencing that made up her cage at the health center. She must have been working unnoticed on that project for a long time. The chimp bent it apart and pulled one strand of the wire through until she could crawl through the fence along with three other chimps.

Jim Post was feeding the animals inside the cage room when he suddenly found himself surrounded by the four escaped chimps. Two of them were extremely dangerous. Jeannie and Toto had both bitten off human fingers and could explode with rage. Jim kept his cool. He walked slowly and deliberately to the cage room door, let himself out, and locked the door behind him. Leaving the chimps secure for the time inside the larger cage room, Jim ran to get help. These chimps were a danger to the several smaller species we were keeping at the time.

Dr. Gale was the only vet at the zoo that day, but he was the best man at animal capture. He was fearless. I started preparing the necessary capture darts—six darts each with enough drugs to bring down a hundred-and-twenty-pound animal. Our plan was to shoot the chimps from outside the cage room through the surrounding chain-link fence. But as soon as they saw the hated capture gun, the wily chimps hid behind any barrier they could find. We were never able to attempt even one shot.

Several men had arrived at the health center in case help was needed. Chimps are too strong to net, four to six times as strong as a man. The capture guns were our only hope. Dr. Gale finally determined we would have to enter the cage room. Looking right at me, he asked, "Who's going in with me?"

"I'm in," I said. I can remember thinking that this was the crisis I had been waiting for to prove my manhood. I felt like I was in a western movie and had just joined the hero in a life or death struggle. Dr. Gale and I took the capture guns. Tony Campo had also volunteered and was backing us up with a rifle in case the chimps charged.

When we unlocked the door, the chimps went crazy. They screamed at the top of their lungs to let us know they were not happy about the capture guns. The elusive animals kept hidden behind every barrier. Finding a position to shoot them was like playing a game of chess. Dr. Gale would send me one way and he would go another looking for a clear shot. I felt afraid but was glad I had volunteered. When I glanced at the men outside the cage, I proudly thought, "the real men were inside."

I finally got a clear shot. I took aim at Jeannie's hind quarter and pulled the trigger. Whoosh, the dart found its mark in the largest section of her thigh. She looked very angry and charged. Dr. Gale and Tony rushed to my aid and we all pointed our guns at the chimp. Jeannie thought better of her action and retreated. We waited in hopes that she would go down and improve our odds. Soon the large chimp was laying flat on her back sound asleep. Three more to go.

We jockeyed for position and were luckily able to scare Toto into an open cage where he whimpered and shook his hands in fear. We shut the door behind him and had only two fairly gentle female chimps left to handle. Still they were agitated and had to be darted. Dr. Gale made a perfect shot on Annie and then I got Bonnie. I can't describe the relief I felt. That was hazardous duty and I knew it. All the patting on the back felt good. At last I felt like a real man—at least for a while.

A MOTHER PYTHON

One day the reptile house called us about an emergency. They had a species of python that lays eggs and then stays around to incubate them. Such behavior is very rare in the world of reptiles. Alligators and crocodiles do, but very rarely snakes. This python not only stays with the eggs but also regularly twitches to raise her body temperature.

This particular female had managed to lay her eggs on gravel and then kept twitching until an underlying heating element had become exposed. Being a dedicated mother with a high threshold of pain, she remained on the heating element until the reptile keepers smelled burning flesh. When they removed her from the cage, they discovered that she had burned a hole six inches by six inches right through the skin on her belly.

They carefully removed the thirty or so eggs and brought mother and eggs to the health center. After initial treatment, we put this fourteen-foot python into a large box in the pharmacy and returned her eggs to her. It was glad reunion. She nuzzled each one and scooted them into a little pile and encircled them. The mother resumed her rhythmic twitching and we all believed there was still a chance to save the babies.

Unfortunately, snakes have a slow metabolism. They move slowly, digest slowly, and *heal* slowly. Daily attention was required to keep the wound clean and the dressing changed. No easy task! Not only was this a large snake capable of killing a man, she was a mother on a mission. Whenever we opened the lid to her cage, she assumed we were after her eggs. God must have given this serpent an above average mothering instinct! When anyone got near her, she would assume a striking position and hiss with rage.

The reptile keepers would jockey for position before they made their lunge. These guys were good and never missed, especially Jay Kilgore. He would firmly grasp her behind the head, and the rest of us would control the body while the doctor treated the wound. If anyone miscalculated even a little, he would end up with rows of massive teeth sunk deeply into his hand. The python is not poisonous, but its bite is both painful and dirty. Snakes are always shedding their teeth so you could be sure several of them would break off and cause massive infections.

After admiring the men who made the dangerous grab for this python's head, I asked if I could try it next time. I felt the need to turn my adventure quotient up a notch. The reptile keepers were very encouraging and assured me there was nothing to it. They coached me ahead of time and warned me about the strength of the snake. I would need to hold on tight or I was sure to get nailed as well as put them in harm's way.

When we removed the lid of the cage, the mother python became tense and alert. She turned her head and examined her adversaries one by one. I felt numb when she stared at me. Like Jay, I moved about to confuse her and get into a position to make the grab. My moment came when she was looking away at another keeper. Now was the perfect time. Unlike my lake jump, there was no room for counting. Dealing with animals called for quick reactions.

Unfortunately I couldn't. I just froze. My mind was screaming, "GRAB!" But my body was saying, "No way, get us out of here!" My body won and suddenly the moment was gone. The python turned and stared directly into my eyes. Everything about her said, "I dare you."

The reptile guys said, "Why don't you watch us another day. You can pick it up later. It's cool. We can't grab wolves and cheetahs and baboons, so don't feel bad about this."

As I backed off for the first time, I felt stripped of manhood. John Wayne would have grabbed her, but I couldn't. I never did. Big, really big snakes seem to bother me. Smaller snakes are okay. I recently owned a nine-foot Burmese python named Jabba and was able to grab him. He bit me one day when I was trying to feed him, but I didn't take it personally. He was just aiming for his food and missed. I sold him the next week.

MY ELUSIVE GOAL

I was almost thirty when it dawned on me that I would always be a boy if I continued to hold on to my definition of manhood. There would always be one more mountain to climb. And with my tendency to volunteer, I was going to fall real good sooner or later! I remember looking at my hands one day and thinking, "Listen, Bud. You still have all your fingers, and you haven't been mauled. There are no big holes where horns have been jammed through your body. So why don't you back off and let the younger guys chase manhood for a while?"

And so I did. Whenever the time came to volunteer for dangerous duty, I started keeping my hands in my pockets. If I couldn't find manhood after seven years on that path, I determined to look for it somewhere else. You wouldn't believe how many guys were standing in line to take my place. They never found manhood, but I did.

The one who had designed human beings had also communicated what it meant to be a man. The truths I began to learn in Scripture did include heroics *if* they were done for unselfish reasons, but heroics were nowhere near the top of the list. What was at the top of the list had to do with good character—things like kindness, honesty, unselfishness, and integrity.

Micah 6:8 delineates manhood as clear as a bell: "He has showed you, O man, what is good. And what does the Lord require of you? To act justly, and to love mercy and walk humbly with your God."

I read in Ecclesiastes 12:13-14, "Now all has been heard; here is the conclusion of the matter: Fear God and keep his commandments, for this is the whole duty of man. For God will bring every deed into judgment, including every hidden thing, whether it is good or evil." Isaiah 66:2 further affirms this assessment. God says, "This is the one I esteem: he who is humble and contrite in spirit, and trembles at my word."

Heroics do have their place. Jesus said, "Greater love has no one than this, that he lay down his life for his friends" (John 15:13). But he was not talking about the kind of Evil Knievel type of heroics I had been aspiring to all my life. Jesus was talking about bravery for the sake of others—not to prove something, but as an expression of an inward reality. This kind of bravery is the by-product of love.

With God, our character is always paramount. That is why he set Moses aside when he was at his John Wayne best and sent him to tend sheep for forty years. After his character had been straightened out, God said, "There is none like my servant Moses."

Pontius Pilate brought Jesus before the people and said, "Behold the Man." He didn't know it, but he was actually introducing to the world everything God intended a man to be. Jesus was a man's man, as well as the ideal man for women. He was brave, good, and kind—the greatest example of unselfishness that the world has ever known.

Now I want to be like him.

2

The Accident

WHEN I WAS EIGHT YEARS OLD, I was asked what I wanted to be... *if* the neighbors let me grow up. It was my neighbor who asked—a fat balding man who looked like he could be related to Alfred Hitchcock. He was forever nursing a cigar while our family lived on East Mendocino Street in Altadena, California.

At that time I wanted to be a paleontologist who studied dinosaurs, looked for their bones, and figured out what they did in their spare time, or find out if they even had spare time. After I answered this man's question, it occurred to me that I should ask why he had said, "if the neighbors let me grow up." He laughed and said, "Well, Gary, you can be a rascal, you know, and some of us on the block try to picture you as an adult and.... Well, it makes you wonder. They study dinosaurs in Africa, don't they?"

"All over, Mr. Alfeld, and in the good old U.S.A. too."

He patted me on the head and said he was just having fun with me. But I understand the question better now than I did thirty-nine years ago. As I think back, there were many adults who were concerned about America's future should I ever come of age. Five years after her retirement, my sixth grade teacher was still asking people who knew me if I was in jail yet. I never went to jail, but I was arrested. I'll explain why later.

FAMILY ROOTS

So much of what we are and how we turn out can be traced back to our parents and families. Let me start with my father. He was really something. Walter Ernest Richmond was born on a cold winter day in January, 1911, in Sioux City, Iowa. His father was a cruel man, both to his wife and to his children.

At a time in history when you just didn't get a divorce, my grandmother Lillian divorced her husband without much ceremony and left town with her baby daughter Maxine. She sadly left her son behind, praying fervently to the Blessed Virgin Mary and saints that her monster of a husband would not in an alcoholic rage kill her son. Times were lean, and Lillian didn't have the slightest clue as to how she would support herself and her daughter. She was not to see my father again for more than fourteen years, but she never stopped loving him or praying for him.

Things did not go well for my father. The lad was beaten daily for minor misdeeds. My grandfather, whom I never met, grew tired of caring for his son and enrolled him in a Catholic boarding school. Perhaps he exaggerated the boy's need for discipline, but the priest in charge simply took over where my grandfather had left off and ordered the nuns to do the same. My father said that he was never without bruises during that period because new ones were inflicted before the old ones had time to heal.

After several weeks my grandfather made a visit to the school on a day when my father had a new crop of bruises on display. He asked my father whether he felt they were deserved and actually believed my father when he said that he did not. My grandfather proceeded to unleash all of his anger on the severe priest and beat him within an inch of his life.

While the priest lay bleeding on the ground, my grandfather yelled, "Nobody but me has the right to leave bruises on the boy the way you did." After he had taken my father back home, he realized that perhaps beating up a priest was not the best way to have handled the situation. He blamed the boy for having inspired his outburst of temper and beat him again.

What do you do when you are twelve years old and your mother has abandoned you and your father seems to hate you? You run away. My father had heard that his mother's sister lived in Astoria, Oregon, with her husband who was not wealthy but comfortable. He heard she was sweet. That seemed to be just what he needed: a good dose of sweet. He simply wanted to be wanted. He hoped that if he traveled more than halfway across a continent, Aunt Addie would want him.

His first night home, my father gathered together a handful of simple treasures, like his pocketknife, watch, three dollars in change, and an extra set of clothes. Then he headed for the train yards where he hoped to hop a freight train bound for the great northwest.

The young boy had the good fortune to run into some men who regularly rode the rails. They helped him into a boxcar where he covered himself with a canvas tarp and waited for the train to take him to the promised land and the imagined warmth of Aunt Addie's legendary love. He stayed on the train until hunger and thirst forced him to get off late in the afternoon of the following day.

Across the endless prairie, my father saw a farmhouse. He started walking toward it in hopes of buying a little food. As he drew near, the evening breeze carried the smell of freshly baked apple pies to his nostrils. The boy's weak knees buckled with the horrible thought that the pie might be denied him. He walked to the kitchen window where the pies had been placed to cool and just stared at them. It occurred to him that perhaps he should grab one and take off, but my father was too honest and just continued to stare.

The farmer's wife noticed the boy staring at her creations and watched him for several minutes. At first she thought the worst and expected him to steal one. But he didn't. He just stared, very much like a well-trained dog that simply will not take his food until his master gives the go-ahead. As the minutes passed her heart softened. She stepped out the back door and said with kindness and grace, "You look like you'd like a piece of pie, young man."

"Yes ma'am, I surely would," answered my father as he fumbled for some change and extended it toward her. "I can pay you, ma'am. I think I would give you everything I have for a piece of your pie. I've not smelled better in my twelve years of life. If I have, it was when I was a baby and I have forgotten, although I cannot imagine a finer smell than this."

"Put your money away, son. You've paid for the pie with an honest heart and kind words, and no more will be required of you. Have you had dinner, son?"

"No ma'am, I haven't."

"Land sakes, son. Go wash your hands and come inside now. My husband's 'bout ready to sit himself down and we can't keep him waiting. When he sits down he means to eat."

My father was directed to the water pump where he washed up as best he could. Then he joined the farmer and his wife at their table. The farmer was quiet and kind, and welcomed my father like he was one of his own.

I loved to hear my father tell this story over and over again when I was young. He described the feast that was set before him that night with such clarity, gratitude, and enthusiasm that I could almost smell and taste it myself. I still remember the menu. There was roast beef, gravy by the ladle, mashed potatoes, green beans, and biscuits so soft and light that they floated an inch or two above the serving basket. There was salad that my dad ate just to be polite, and of course the best apple pie he had ever had or would ever have as it turned out. He downed three pieces, which was all he could hold.

When he was full, the couple could no longer contain their curiosity. The farmer inquired, "Son, it ain't a bit our business you see, but the Mrs. and I are wondering what you're doing out here on the prairie. We don't get visitors your age much. Actually you're the first one ever."

"I'm trying to get to my Aunt Addie's in Astoria, Oregon. My mother died in childbirth in nineteen and twenty-two, and my daddy died of consumption last month. I run away from the orphanage because I know things will go better for me if I make it to my aunt's house. She loves children and from what my mom used to say about her, she's the kind what will always have room for one more." That's about as much truth as my dad felt like he could tell at that point. He didn't want to risk having the couple contact his father. He would rather have died than go back to him.

The couple nodded but didn't ask any more questions, then asked the boy to spend the night. The feather bed beat the boxcar three ways till next Tuesday, and my father woke up to the smell of bacon and eggs, hash browns, and more biscuits. When my father left that morning, he had a sack full of food along with a hug and a handshake to send him on his journey. I think he would have gladly stayed to become their son, but they didn't ask, so he kept going.

AUNT ADDIE'S LOVE

He found the spot where he had set off from the railroad tracks the previous afternoon and followed them west by northwest. Soon he hopped a freight train once again and watched the prairie speed by at forty miles per hour. For two days he had no idea where he was going. He didn't even know what state he was seeing as he stared out of the warm and humid confines of the boxcar.

The prairie gave way to great stands of trees. Though he didn't realize it, he crossed from Wyoming into Idaho while he was lifting his nose to enjoy the forest fragrance and beauty of the Salmon River. Providence was on his side, for the train would rest the next morning in the booming logging community of Astoria—the end of the line for the train, but the beginning of better days for my father. While my dad slept, the train entered Oregon and followed the mighty Columbia River to the coast.

The boy was roused awake by a rude conductor who cussed him out for being a stowaway and pushed him out of the boxcar. When my dad asked where they were, the conductor said, "We're at the end of the line, boy—Astoria, Oregon. If this isn't where you were going, you're out of luck, because when this train turns around tomorrow it's just going where you already been. So whatta you gotta say about that?"

"This *is* where I was going, sir. I just have to find my Aunt Addie and Uncle Delmer." My dad had a big smile on his face. Even though he was tired, hungry, and almost broke, he was full of hope as he thanked the conductor for the information. He thought to himself, "Pretty good for a twelve-year-old boy. All you have to do is find your Aunt Addie, then things will get a whole lot better." My father had carried her address halfway across the United States, and Astoria was not that big. He didn't know it, but he was less than four miles from his aunt's house. He received good directions from several people who seemed to be pretty friendly, and in no time he was standing outside Aunt Addie's door. He had never met her but everything he had ever heard was good. "She loves everybody and everybody loves her," was the phrase that he had heard at least a hundred times.

As he stood staring at the house, for the first time since he left Iowa he was not glad. He was afraid. What if she didn't want him? Nobody else did—even his own mother. What right did he have to expect she would take him in? What would he do if she didn't?

My father knew he had no choice. His feet were heavy as he climbed the stairs. He had a river of tears bottled up inside of him, but nobody had ever given him permission to cry. He knocked at the door, and it seemed as if he turned fourteen before it was answered. The door opened slowly and there in the doorway stood a very kind-looking lady about thirty years of age. Her hair was in a bun, and she was dressed in the conservative style of 1923.

"May I help you, son?" the lady asked softly.

"Are you my Aunt Addie?" said my father, his voice quivering.

The lady lifted both hands to her mouth and said, "That depends. Are you Lillian's boy Walter?"

"Yes, ma'am, I am."

"I'm your aunt." She put both hands on my dad's shoulders and looked at him for several moments. "You are Lil's son for sure. You look like her, don't you?" Then she embarrassed the boy by pulling him close to her breast. My father choked back tears. He didn't want her to think he was a baby, but he did hug back and could have stayed that way much longer if he had been allowed. The boy knew everything was going to be all right. He had done the right thing.

Uncle Delmer turned out to be as open and as willing to take my father in as Aunt Addie. In fact, nothing that had been said about them had been exaggerated. They loved everybody and everybody loved them. My father loved them, that was for sure. Every time their name was mentioned during my childhood, he would smile. Addie had finished his upbringing as if he were her own.

For whatever reason, his mother never made contact with her sister. Nobody ever asked her why, but there was an unspoken understanding that Lillian was ashamed of having failed at her marriage and just couldn't face the disappointment of her relatives. Such were the times. Divorce was frowned on inside and outside of the church in the twenties.

Sensing that he was a financial burden to his aunt and uncle, my father dropped out of school after ninth grade and never went back. He apprenticed as a lumberjack at a nearby logging camp and by sixteen could handle an axe or a crosscut saw as well as anyone. The lad brought home a salary to be proud of. It meant a lot to him to pay his way, or carry his own load, as he put it.

It was in the logging camps that he learned how to play poker. He became very good at it. Lady Luck was only a part of the game. Using good judgment and knowing a bit about human nature could tip the scales a good bit. In no time he was supplementing his salary with his winnings from the nightly poker games.

My father believed what P.T. Barnum once said. "There is a sucker born every day." He found that suckers could be taken to the cleaners anytime they were invited. Once he had learned the pay days at the various logging camps, he became buddies with the men in those camps who neglected to use good judgment. He also looked for men who drank heavily, since they especially could be picked clean in a poker game. My dad would bring liquor by the case to games and only invite men with little skill and drinking problems to play with him.

I asked him if he won much money from these men. He laughed and put his arm on my shoulder. "Son, it was like taking candy from a baby. I made so much money I quit being a lumberjack and just played poker. It was a lot easier than cutting trees, and I made a bundle."

"Why'd ya quit, Dad?" I was curious as to why he had taken up plastering—an equally brutal way to make a living—when he could get rich fleecing suckers.

I'll never forget what he said. "Taking candy from babies don't make you feel good after awhile. I used to wonder what happened when the men I'd gotten drunk went home to their wives and children and told them they lost their paychecks. I had to live with myself, and I couldn't do it when I was playing poker. Plastering is real hard work, but it's honest and you can go back years from now and see folks living in homes you built. I have something to show for what I do now that I can be proud of later. And son, there's something to say for a clear conscience."

MISTAKES ALONG THE WAY

My father didn't go from gambling straight to plastering. There was a middle step. He joined the Navy. I really don't know a lot about this period, but what I do is a kick. And the funny thing is I just found this out one month ago from a cousin I hadn't seen in over thirty years.

My father had joined the Navy in the early thirties while the world was at peace, but taking orders was not his cup of tea. He only enjoyed himself on shore leave when he could chase women and get drunk out of his skull. It was on one of these shore leaves that he was smitten by a girl that was "a looker," but not the kind to write home about. Before a weekend leave was over, my father had married her and had her face tattooed on the upper part of his left arm. Under her face was written her name, "Boots."

I asked about that tattoo just once. I said, "Dad, who was Boots?" He scowled at me and answered, "She was a bad mistake I made on a weekend a long time ago. Don't ask me anything more about her."

I didn't, but I looked at that tattoo thousands of times and wondered. And one day last month I finally understood why my dad had said what he did. Boots soon made it clear that she didn't like the idea that he had to go back to the Navy, so soon after they were married my father didn't go back. He just went A.W.O.L.—which could have gotten him shot had a war been going on. He gave himself up and spent time in the jail. During that time Boots divorced him, leaving my dad with a broken heart, a jail term, and a tattoo that refused to fade a shade for the rest of his life.

When he got out of jail he moved to Southern California where there were lots of jobs, good weather, and lots of good-looking women. He settled in and developed a pretty regular drinking habit to help him relax after work. He hit the bar almost every evening. There he met my mother, Henrietta Fultz, who had also been married less than a year and was divorced.

While they were dating my dad's father showed up one day after years of silence, having gotten my father's address from Aunt Addie. In an effort to be reconciled, my father invited him to move in with him. But before two months were up, my grandfather's old anger flared. He left in a rage late one night and was never seen or heard from by anyone in the family again. I never did meet him.

Henrietta married Walter when she was twenty and he was thirty. Barely a year passed before they gave birth to my older brother Steve. The baby was delivered by Cesarean section, and the birth nearly killed my mother. The doctors advised her to have her fallopian tubes tied because they were convinced that she could not survive another pregnancy. They tied those tubes tight, and my parents were the proud owners of an only child.

Four years later my mother became worried about her health. She began vomiting every morning and experienced cravings, unexplained cravings. She laughed that whatever the illness, it was just like being pregnant—which was of course impossible because her tubes had been tied.

Well, surprise, surprise. The doctor had never received his merit badge for knot tying. Or else he had been distracted and tied a slip knot instead of a square knot, because there I was, very small but growing fast.

RAINY DAYS WITH A LITTLE SUNSHINE

But that's how things had worked out for my mother her whole life—always different than she had planned. Her real father had been killed during the First World War. Her mother had remarried a dapper Dan who had been a professional baseball player with the Philadelphia Athletics. He was a fantastic grandfather to me but a neglectful and demeaning stepfather to my mother. He was also an alcoholic and an unfaithful husband. My grandparents stayed together until my grandmother died of cancer. To his credit my grandfather took tender care of my grandmother until the day she died. Then he remarried two months later and died in his late eighties still chasing women in bars.

I know nothing about my mother's brief first marriage other than that she "married a bum"—as my grandfather put it. He was glad the bum left and hoped never to see him again. Our family didn't talk much about mistakes they made, so I've always had to learn the hard way. All my mother would ever share about the old days was that she had had an unhappy childhood. I could tell that her bad memories were connected to my grandfather. Her glances, her facial expressions, her lack of conversation with him all added up. When you put alcoholic, critical, unfaithful, and absent together you can sort of understand. What it added up to was she never really had a dad. The effects were visible to me all the years of my life. She was rarely happy. I would describe her life like the weather in Oregon: rainy days interrupted by brief periods of sunshine.

So there I was in her womb. I was unplanned, unneeded, unwanted, a threat to her very life and the biggest surprise— more like shock—my mother was ever to receive. I was delivered by Cesarean section on August 29, 1944, at Doctor's Hospital in what was then a nice section of downtown Los Angeles. It is now a war zone infested with gangs killing each other.

My parents named me before they got to know me, thank goodness. They called me Gary Michael Richmond. Gary means "friend in battle" and Michael means "the shining one." I like my name. If they had gotten to know me first, they would have drawn from another list. I don't think I would have liked Bozo or Trouble or Storm. Those were on the list that best described my early days.

In recounting my birth, which my mother did often in large gatherings, I was always referred to as "an accident." She further described me as unplanned and a handful.

Can you remember what it is like to view life as a child? I do. I remember how I saw myself during my first ten years of life. I viewed myself in terms of how I understood the word *accident*—like what happens when automobiles crash into each other or what a baby or young child does if he or she is not yet potty trained.

When I was capable of abstract thinking, I came to realize I was not an accident. I was more of a divine practical joke or judgment. I was a minor miracle, and that has always given me a sense of being born for a reason. Despite everyone's efforts and plans, I had come on the scene. Even before I knew anything about a personal God, I figured he wanted me here for a reason. I may have been unplanned from my parents' perspective, but God had plans for me. Way down deep I've always thought it was he who untied the knot that set me free.

I haven't always been on speaking terms with God. But he always knew me and watched over me as I grew up. I can look back now and understand he was always there, because if he hadn't been I would never have made it this far! This is my story of coming of age, whenever that occurred. Some think I'm still coming of age. Join me in my first true-life adventure.

3

Ladybug

WHEN I WAS SEVEN our family got a small black and tan puppy and named her Ladybug. I can still vividly recall the warmth of her head laying across my bare feet or the look of love in her eyes. Ladybug would always watch to see if she would be invited on any adventure that crossed the boundaries of our yard. An ardent traveler who loved to ride in the car, no dog ever enjoyed more the wind whipping her ears and flapping her lips. She would lean as far as she could out the back window of our '51 Chevrolet station wagon.

Ladybug weighed in at about fifteen pounds, maybe twenty. Most believed that she was a cross between a cocker spaniel and a beagle. She was a happy dog and ticklish. If you scratched her in just the right place she actually smiled. Now, I know that's hard to believe and doesn't sound scientific or enlightened. But, hang it all, this dog smiled. If you saw it, you would call it that too.

When I was young I actually thought of her as a member of the family, the youngest child. To me she was Ladybug Richmond. She slept with us, and many was the morning that I was licked awake. Between my seventh and ninth year, I never washed my ears because Ladybug did it for me almost every morning.

She did have one fault that remained with her all the days

of her life: breath that you could see on a warm day. Whatever doggy breath is, Ladybug had twice as much as should be allotted, and we had to apologize for it more than once. She also possessed a great capacity for natural gas production!

Ladybug was my friend and shadow. I always loved her but never more than the one summer day before seventh grade when I had to ask for her forgiveness. Here is what happened.

I was raised in Altadena, California, a small friendly town nestled against the San Gabriel mountains—the very mountains that serve as the backdrop to the Rose Parade or the Rose Bowl. The San Gabriels watch over Pasadena and Altadena and most of the Los Angeles basin.

Of all that Altadena had to commend it, smack dab in the middle of the "amen corner" was Kern's Delicatessen. Old Mr. Kern served some of the finest culinary delights known to the palates of our species. His swiss cheese, pumpernickel bread, and kosher dill pickles were the best. I gladly made the four-block walk to the deli anytime some benefactor would finance the pilgrimage.

One very hot summer afternoon in deep August, I suddenly remembered how much I enjoyed biting into one of Mr. Kern's reknowned kosher dills. My brother and a couple of friends all agreed to go. When we got to the front door, Ladybug was wiggling with delight at the prospect of coming along with us. We were soon on our way to the gates of heaven.

We did not keep Ladybug on a leash because she would never bite anyone. She was always bounding just ahead, stopping now and then to smell something and make a memory. She always made these walks a game and would run over and jump on us now and then to let us know she was glad to be part of the adventure. When we arrived at Kern's, we told Ladybug to sit at the front door and wait for us while we ate inside.

Life doesn't get better than eating at Kern's Delicatessen with family and friends. I purchased one slice of pumpernickel bread, one slice of aged swiss cheese, one large kosher dill pickle, and a bottle of Dad's Old Fashioned Root Beer. We left only after licking everything off of our fingers.

Once outside we ordered Ladybug to follow us home. Twenty steps down the street we peered through the Hillcrest Pharmacy window and noticed the latest issue of *Mad Magazine*. We again ordered Ladybug to sit on the sidewalk and wait for us while we went in the store. We all read *Mad* over my friend's shoulder and laughed at the absurd humor, tears streaming down our faces. Finally, the store clerk asked us to buy or fly so we left—a little embarrassed and a little miffed— through the back door which provided a short cut home. We also left Ladybug waiting patiently at the front door of Hillcrest Pharmacy.

On the way home we groused over being given the bum's rush. The afternoon began to blend with evening and our friends both left for home and dinner. My dad came home from a hard day's work, and after washing up called us to the dinner table. It was a meat and potatoes meal, with the kind of leftovers any family dog would kill for. My father scraped them onto a plate and stepped out the back door to call for Ladybug.

When she didn't come, he asked us if we had seen her. We just looked at each other. I didn't know for sure what Steve was going to do, but I was trying to figure out a way to blame our thoughtless mistake on *him*. I refused to answer my dad's question, hoping that my brother would get most of the blame for losing our dog. Steve finally admitted that we had left her outside the pharmacy. My father had a disgusted look that he directed at both of us.

He told us to jump in the car and backed out of our driveway a lot faster than usual. He didn't say much, except to inquire if we had traded our brains for sawdust. We knew better than to answer that particular question. If we said no we were smart-mouthing; if we said yes we were smart-mouthing. So we both did what he wanted; we looked guilty and stupid and kept quiet. Now I don't know what you're thinking, but don't give a button to modern psychology's notion that there are not appropriate times to tongue-lash someone. God did it all the time to Israel, and Jesus did it to his disciples. Steve and I were getting less than we deserved. I knew it then and I know it now.

My father knew enough about dogs to know that Ladybug was capable of following her own scent home, so he followed the route we had walked to the delicatessen. We didn't see her, and the farther we drove, the worse I felt. I had let down one of my best friends. A lump stuck in my throat as I began to picture my dog run over by a car or cringing in the back of a cage at the dog pound. We finally rounded the corner of Mariposa Lane and Lake Street and saw a small dark form curled into a ball by the front door of the pharmacy.

Steve stuck his head out the window and yelled, "Here, girl!" His yell awakened her, and she bounced against the glass thinking we were still in the store. Steve got out of the car and picked her up. I have never witnessed a more emotional reunion. Ladybug wiggled until I thought she would fall apart. She whined happily all the way home and licked every hand that came within a foot of her.

My father was happy about the outcome. "All's well that ends well, but don't you ever let that happen to your dog again. I don't have to tell you all the bad things that could have happened to her, do I?" We agreed that he didn't.

That night I asked Ladybug if she wanted to sleep with me. Her tail wagged and she ran ahead of me and jumped up on the bed. When I turned out the light I called her to come close. I hugged her and told her how sorry I was to have let her down. She just kissed me and rolled over to have me scratch her tummy. I did that until we both fell asleep.

Ladybug was always anxious to forgive. All that was really important to her was that she was a part of a family, our family, her family. The saying that dogs are a man's best friend really isn't so far off, at least in my experience.

4

The Black Widow

THE GREATEST LESSON I EVER LEARNED from animals was not learned at the zoo. It was in a mossy, moldy greenhouse in the backyard of a lady I was sure was a witch. I was eight years old at the time.

Spring was just giving way to summer, and keeping the grass green between waterings was becoming increasingly difficult. School was almost out and I was looking forward to three months of running barefoot through a creative string of adventures. My mother was just beginning to fix dinner when the afternoon stillness was broken by the persistent ring of the front doorbell. At the door stood an older man. His tie was loosened and he was drenched with perspiration. He wiped the sweat from his forehead and began his presentation, one that he had probably given fifty times before coming to our front door.

"Hello, ma'am. My name is Edgar Beasly and I'm from the health department. We are going door-to-door to alert people to the fact that they need to spray for black widow spiders. I bet you have already noticed that there are more spiders than usual this year. Doctors are reporting many bites that they feel are probably black widow bites. Last week a little girl nearly died from one. So we're here to warn you that we are having an epidemic of black widow spiders. This sometimes happens after a real wet spring."

He handed my mother a pamphlet and said, "Ma'am, here's a pamphlet that gives you some real important information about black widows. It shows you what they look like and more importantly what their webs look like. We'd sure be much obliged if you'd spray."

When Mr. Beasly left, my mother scanned the pamphlet and then stared at me with legitimate concern. "Gary, if I ever catch you so much as walking by a black widow spider web, I'll spank your back side shiny. Do you understand me, young man?"

I nodded that I did and then she handed me the pamphlet. I was fascinated. On the cover was a menacing picture of a large female black widow posed to reveal the red hourglass on the underside of her shiny black abdomen. It made note that she lived in an irregular web that would likely be found in dark places like garages, wood piles, and under cabinets.

The section that most caught my interest was entitled, "The Bite of the Black Widow Spider." The possible symptoms were listed as discoloration at the site of the bite, nausea, a severe headache, unusual swelling, labored breathing, and blurred vision. The pamplet warned that some children even died from the bite of the black widow spider.

My mother never realized that she had just provided a road map for my next great adventure: a black widow safari. I couldn't wait to tell my close friend Doug Sigler about the greatest idea of my life.

"Now here it is, Doug. On Saturday morning my parents will be gone for three hours. I figure that will give us time to catch ten black widow spiders. We can take those bandits down to Elliot Junior High School and dump them on this red ant hill that I located. It will be great. The red ants will come streaming out to protect their home and there will be a scary fight. The red ants will win, and we will have done our part in Altadena's battle to fight the black widows."

"What if we get bit?" Doug asked.

"We're not going to let those child-killers get us. We'll be real careful. Hey, you're not going to chicken out on me, are you?"

"Well, no," Doug answered defensively.

I made Doug take the bloodbrother handshake and promise not to tell any living soul what we were going to do at 8:30 a.m. Saturday morning. He took it knowing that if he broke it, his teeth and hair would fall out. We got a peanut butter jar and poked holes in its lid. We didn't want any of the spiders dying before they got a chance to fight the red ants. We chose a two-foot long stick for catching the spiders and hid our safari gear behind the garage for safekeeping.

When Saturday came and my parents had left on their shopping trip, I ran to Doug's house. He was already waiting for me in his front yard. We grabbed our gear and headed for my backyard. I had already located several webs. On the way there we ran into another good friend, Eric, who was coming over to see if we could play. We finally decided that we'd better let him in on our secret but made him take an even more solemn oath than Doug's.

"What kind of oath?" asked Eric.

"The kind that if you break it something scary happens."

Eric really wanted in so he took the oath.

"I, Eric."

"I, Eric."

"Promise never to tell about the black widow safari."

"Promise never to tell about the black widow safari."

"If I do the devil will make my mother's hair fall out."

"What?"

"You heard me, Eric. Do you want in or not?"

"It's just that I don't want the devil around my mom!"

"Are you planning to tell someone?"

"No."

"Then you don't have anything to worry about. There's a reason for this, Eric. You're not very good at keeping secrets, and this will help you."

"Okay," said Eric. "If I do the devil will make my mother's hair fall out."

"That wasn't so bad, was it?" asked Doug.

We walked down our long overgrown driveway and ran right into my twelve-year-old brother, Steve. Before we could stop him, Eric blurted out, "Guess what, Steve? We're going to catch ten black widow spiders and dump them on a red ant hill. Isn't that neat?"

My brother then treated us to the words we least liked to hear. "You guys are too young!" Boy, I hated those words. Steve still thought it sounded like a great idea and offered to catch the spiders for us. If we were good he would let us hold the jar. As we followed my brother to our backyard, I held up my fist to Eric and said, "I'm never going to tell you a secret again. I hope you're thinking about what you just did to your mother, you oathbreaker."

I sadly handed over the catching-stick to my brother, and Doug reluctantly handed the peanut butter jar to me. Eric was trying to visualize his mother bald and wondering if she would know that it was his fault.

It took only a minute to discover the first spider. It was residing behind our tool shed. Her web was spun between the fence and the shed and bore the evidence of many a successful hunt. The dried bodies of three moths and two flies were mute reminders of her deadly venom.

We crowded behind my brother Steve to watch him catch the first black widow. After he managed to get her on the end of the stick, I opened the jar with trembling hands. A tap of the stick yielded its first prisoner. The spider was medium-sized and looked none too happy about being caught. She looked just like the spider on the pamphlet and when I lifted the jar we were able to see the bright red hourglass on her shiny black abdomen.

As the jar began to fill up my job became difficult. The fifth spider attached a web to the lid so that when I opened the jar for the sixth spider, I pulled the fifth across my hand. After we had caught eight spiders we faced a dilemma. We had run out of spiders to catch on our property. Steve wanted to stop at eight but I insisted that we had agreed to catch ten. Steve gave in but had no idea as to where we should hunt next.

Eric, who had been the quiet observer on the safari, made a great suggestion. "I bet the evil queen of the black widow spiders lives in Mrs. Brown's greenhouse." Mrs. Brown lived next door to Doug, and all the neighborhood children were really afraid of her. She hated small children and would call the police if they set foot on her property. Some of us were convinced that she was a witch and could cast spells that would keep you under her power.

Eric's idea seemed so attractive because catching the spiders had become too easy. Besides, my brother Steve was having all the fun. It was such a great idea that we forgave Eric for breaking his oath. He was glad. He just couldn't get used to the idea of having a bald mother. He thought it might be embarrassing.

Doug suggested that we sneak onto Mrs. Brown's property from his adjoining backyard. In fact her greenhouse was in the very back of her yard so Doug's suggestion made good sense. We peered over his fence into the untrimmed jungle that covered her yard and concluded that she was not outside. One at a time we dropped into forbidden territory and slipped silently into the greenhouse.

It was damp and dark, musty and moldy, perfect for black widows. Fearing Mrs. Brown would jump out and grab us at any minute, we asked Eric to keep watch.

Underneath her gardening bench was a red clay pot, the five-gallon kind you would use for a small palm tree. It was turned upside down and resting on three red bricks. Steve and Doug turned it over very slowly and carefully. We each drew in our breath at what we saw. At the bottom of that clay pot was the largest black widow we had ever seen. She was fat and seemed to be throbbing with poison. She was protecting her silky white eggsack, and unlike the other spiders was simply not afraid of the stick.

After considerable effort Steve was able to get the deadly giant on the end of the stick. He called for me to open the jar. I shook the jar until I was able to count the eight captured spiders and carefully removed the lid from the jar. My hands were trembling as Steve brought the stick to the mouth of the jar. Just at the moment he was going to tap, the spider made a jump for it. She landed right between my bare feet. I backed away from the escaping menace and in the excitement forgot to put the lid back on the jar. I watched with rapt attention as my brother struggled to get the spider back on the stick.

I failed to notice that a medium-sized female was crawling on the back of my hand. I slowly became aware of an eerie sensation and stared in disbelief at the little killer that was taking a morning walk on me. The jar slipped through my fingers and black widows began to run everywhere. They mattered little anymore. The game was over. I was unable to speak anything meaningful but I managed a pretty good sound—something like, **"YAAAAA!"**

My brother looked at me with fear in his eyes too, but our fear was different. For the first time in my life I really believed that I was going to die. Not like in cowboys and Indians where you could get up again, but like everything going dark and after that, I wasn't sure. It took all my strength to keep from fainting. I could feel every step the spider took on the back of my hand. I stayed perfectly still.

My tear-filled eyes begged my brother to please get the spider off my hand. His index finger assumed a flicking position within an inch of the spider. I held my breath and wanted to close my eyes, but I was afraid that if I did it would be for the last time. The spider stopped as if to consider what threat the finger posed. When she did, Steve flicked with all his might. The spider went flying.

I have never felt a greater sense of relief in my life. Neither have I ever learned a more important truth: *someday I am going to die.* How you feel about that truth has everything to do with how you prepare for it. Without any belief in God or a future existence, it really doesn't matter how you live your life. But if you do believe in God, then everything we do probably matters.

Two verses in the Bible really intrigue me. One is, "... it is appointed for men to die once and after this comes judgment...." (Heb 9:27). We were designed to die. To die once is part of what being a human being is all about. We have an appointment with death, and nothing we can do will make us early or late.

The other verse in James concerns his view of life and death. "Come now, you who say, 'Today or tomorrow, we shall go to such and such a city, and spend a year there and engage in business and make a profit.' Yet you do not know what your life will be like tomorrow. You are just a vapor that appears for a little while and vanishes away. Instead you ought to say, 'If the Lord wills we shall live and do this or that'" (Jas 4:13-15).

Scripture clearly teaches that there is a God and what we do matters a great deal to him. It also makes clear that whatever we're going to accomplish needs to be completed before we die. The wisest man who ever lived wrote a dissertation on his search for truth and wisdom. He concludes with these words: "The end of the matter; all has been heard. Fear God and keep his commandments; for this is the whole duty of man. For God will bring every deed into judgment, with every secret thing, whether good or evil" (Eccl 12:13-14).

5

Mrs. West Didn't Like Me Very Much

MRS. WEST WAS THE GREATEST sixth grade teacher in the world, *if* you were one her favorites. I was not. I wasn't even in the top ten. If Adolph Hitler, Charles Manson, or Saddam Hussein had been sixth graders in her class in 1955, I sincerely think they would have topped me on her most-favored list.

Since Mrs. West didn't like me, I didn't like her back. I'm not proud now of all the things I did to earn her wrath, but I was ten. Now that I have grown up, I could never again treat anyone else that way. So this part of my story is kind of a written confession. No teacher really deserved to have a student like me in class. At the time, however, I believed Mrs. West deserved everything I did and more.

By the time I got to fifth grade, Mrs. West was in the twilight of her career. (She may have thought of that year with me as the Twilight Zone.) Her shoulder length, silver-gray hair was streaked with blond here and there. At age sixty-two, she had the appearance of longing for a drink from that lake they call "Retirement," but she still had two more years to teach.

51

When Mrs. West would ask us to work quietly, her mind seemed to be far away, maybe as far as Tahiti or Europe—or wherever you go when you don't really want to be where you are. Her eyes looked tired most of the time and revealed that she had more memories than dreams. She seemed to be marking time with every lunch bell, every recess, and every weekend. These were sign posts telling her that her journey, her quest, perhaps her promise was almost but not quite fulfilled.

Her face wore the effects of her journey. Under her eyes were dark folds of skin, shopping bags as far as bags go. Crow's feet marked the corners of her eyes. To tell you the truth, the crow didn't stop with her eyes but just flat stomped all over her face.

The aging process rested on Mrs. West like a tick on a dog. She seemed to have a lot of wrinkles for a sixty-two-year-old teacher. (Kids can sure do that to a person!) One of our jokes was, "I bet she has to file through her wrinkles to find her mouth." That was especially funny because her mouth was very large. Mrs. West wore a lot of makeup in an effort to hide the effects of time, but it was sort of a wasted effort. Her lipstick was too dark and she wore too much rouge.

Her smile revealed teeth that were yellow and darkening with time. Mrs. West seemed only to smile for two reasons: when she was with her favorites and when she was humiliating those of us who were not her pets. I seemed to be her best reason to smile because I got into trouble a lot. She seemed to take deep and abiding pleasure in humiliating me in hopes that I might reform my behavior.

We got started off on the wrong foot. When we first met, I said, "Hi, Mrs. West. My name is Gary Richmond, and my brother Steve was in your class four years ago."

She squinted as she searched her mind, then looked hard

into my eyes and studied my facial features. "You look like your brother, don't you know! If you are anything like your brother, you and I will get along famously. He was quiet as I remember." As she fingered a prominent mole on her chin, just for a second she reminded me of the witch in Snow White.

I didn't like being told that I looked just like my brother because at the time I didn't *like* my brother. I really didn't have any good reason, but Mark Twain put his finger smack dab in the middle of the matter when he said, "There is no greater annoyance than the annoyance of a good example." That was my brother, good old, good example Steve. He always did what he was told when he was told to do it. Because Steve was such a good boy, I stood out as the opposite to my parents and to my grandparents and neighbors.

Not that I *wanted* to be called a good boy. I wanted to be *me*, to have fun doing what *I* wanted to do when *I* wanted to do it. To my mind, Steve was lackluster, boring, the color gray, a still winter day, an old dusty book, a worn-out pair of pajamas. Mrs. West wanted me to be just like my brother! She thought I looked just like him! I was in trouble, and she needed new glasses.

That was another thing. Mrs. West wore those glasses that were too fancy, the kind with little wings that stuck out at the side and were decorated with rhinestones. When she wasn't reading, they would hang just below her chest by a sterling silver chain. They dangled in space and swung back and forth—drawing attention to the glasses and her chest. There were lots of times I would be staring at her glasses which were swaying hypnotically, only to raise my eyes and find Mrs. West glaring at me. She probably thought that I had been staring at her chest, but I couldn't think of a way to defend myself.

SIXTH-GRADE HUMOR

I liked to talk when I was eleven, and I wasn't always prudent about when I talked. It was usually when Mrs. West was talking. My mouth probably caused her the greatest anguish. She pretty much talked most of the time so you either talked to someone when she was talking or you waited until recess. I could never wait that long. I was sure I would forget what I was going to say, and I usually considered what I was going to say pretty important.

Mrs. West had quite an arsenal of punishments for various offenses, but she always started you out on the same one. If you talked when she talked, you got to write "I will learn to be a quiet student" one hundred times. You wrote on that old school paper that had the chunks of wood in it, and you did it during recess. I missed a lot of recesses. If you laid all of my sentences side-by-side, they might go halfway to the moon, maybe a third.

I have always tried to be funny, and when you're in the sixth grade, humor is still fairly primitive. It really doesn't take much more than primal eruptions from body openings to crack the guys up and embarrass the girls, so I belched a lot because it was the most tasteful of the eruptions. I would wait until it was really quiet and Mrs. West wasn't looking. Then I belched.

It usually got a pretty good laugh, at least at first. When I was young I was very inclined to go too far. As the laughs diminished, my gastric eruptions got louder and more disruptive. My closest friends Doug Sigler, Willie Forsythe, Bodie Hull, and Joe Pechnace never ceased laughing at my daily antics. Early on it was popular for the whole class not to tell Mrs. West that I was the explosive offender. But, I became a nuisance and a lot of the kids got tired of my showing off.

Little Ynez Taggert, Miss Teacher's Pet 1955-56, finally answered Mrs. West's question, "Who in the world made that rude sound?"

"Gary Richmond did, Mrs. West, and I for one am getting sick of it," said the prissy little teacher's pet. "Make him stop, Mrs. West. He makes me want to vomit!"

"You can count on my putting a stop to it, Miss Taggert," said Mrs. West, as she put the end of her fancy glasses between her teeth and thought what to do. "Gary, you stay after class at lunch today," she hissed. She had the same smile that the witch in *The Wizard of Oz* had when she said to Dorothy, "I'll get you, my pretty." I felt uncomfortable.

When the kids all filed out to lunch, I sat quietly waiting for her to do whatever she wanted to do. She sat with her face to the window. Leaning fully back in her chair, she rocked slightly and tapped her number two yellow pencil nervously on the desk. Five minutes passed, and I could feel my stomach curling into a knot. I knew she wasn't going to kill me or anything, but there are worse things than death to a sixth grader. Mrs. West was old enough to know about them. They involved humiliation in front of your peers. She was not beyond humiliating someone who had rung her chimes. She was breathing deeply—the kind of breathing that you do when you are trying to stay under control, like not losing your temper or your mind. Finally she stood up.

"Do you know what you are?" Mrs. West asked with controlled rage. Then she waited for me to answer. You had to be careful with how you answered her. If you answered the wrong way, there was a mighty good chance that she'd blow up. I was sitting very close to her and if she blew, I knew she'd take me with her and I wasn't ready to go. What was I, I wondered. What was she looking for? Something bad, I reasoned. So I humbly answered, "I'm a bad boy," hoping that would satisfy whatever need she had to see me humble myself.

"You're that, too and much more. You're a nuisance, a pest, a distraction. You're a raspberry seed in my wisdom tooth, a constant annoying drip of water. You are a monkey wrench in the spokes of human progress and in all my years of teaching you take the cake for being a bother."

Well, I thought to myself, that sure beats the heck out of bad boy. Did you ever have one of those moments when you weren't quite sure how to feel? That was one of those moments for me. Way down deep what she said hurt my feelings because I wanted her to like me, to care about me. On the other hand, she didn't like me, that was a fact. And I didn't like her. So it was sort of satisfying to know that I had gotten to her in a big way.

Kids don't think cumulatively, so I thought she was overreacting to one silly belch. Our eyes met and I tried to look penitent and humble because I was hungry and wanted to go to lunch and tell Doug and Bodie that I had taken the cake at being a bother to Mrs. West. That was not to be.

"Young man, you will not be going to recess for awhile. You will stay behind when the others have gone and write on the board neatly and clearly five hundred times, "I have not been a good citizen." When you have completed the task, we will talk about your privileges. Do you understand the assignment, Gary?"

"Yes."

"Do you have any questions?"

"Yes."

"What?!"

"How do you spell citizen?"

Her eyes narrowed and her jaw muscles tightened as she took a three-by-five card and wrote out in bold letters, "I have not been a good citizen." Mrs. West waved it at me as if she was going to say something, then handed it to me and said,

"Write it five hundred times just like that. You may eat your lunch and begin."

I wolfed down my lunch and went to the blackboard with just ten minutes left of lunch. I began to write. I wrote as fast as I could because I wanted the punishment to be over so that I would be able to go to recess. There were a lot of people I would rather spend my time with than Mrs. West—including everyone I had ever met and most of the villains in all the movies I had ever seen.

When the lunch bell rang I counted the sentences I had written in ten minutes. Forty! That meant that in one hundred minutes I would write four hundred sentences. Then it would take me twenty-five more minutes to write one hundred more. Every day we had two recesses and one lunch, so if it took me ten minutes to eat my lunch, I figured I would be able to write forty minutes a day. That meant being confined with Mrs. West for three days and one recess. That's a long time to spend with someone you don't like.

We had blackboards on two full walls and they began to fill up with the message that I was not a good citizen. I was sort of embarrassed when the class came back in and considered my progress. There was a bit of teasing from some of the girls, but when a couple of the boys made a joke about my punishment, my friend Bodie told them to shut up if they didn't want a nose all over their face. He warned them, "Gary and me are buddies. Don't mess with my buddy." I liked Bodie. He was the kind of friend that sticks by you no matter which way the wind is blowing.

My arm grew tired and my progress slowed. My shoulder grew sore and what I thought would be a three-day-plus-one-recess assignment stretched into four full days. The blackboard had to be erased a lot to make room for the five hundred sentences. The two walls screamed out their disapproval of my personhood. I pretty much kept my head down most of the time because I was tired of the punishment and the glaring reminder that I was a bad citizen.

Mrs. West was winning whatever battle of wills was taking place. I certainly didn't think that I would belch again soon. I was silenced. My wings were clipped. My undaunted spirit was wounded, and I was beaten. I guessed that the dye was cast. I would have to be a good citizen. The thought of it broke my heart and took the color out of my cheeks.

The moment finally came when I wrote the last sentence, but I did not do so gladly. That meant that Mrs. West and I would have a little talk. I finished writing and slid into my chair. Then I said, "Mrs. West, I'm finished." She was correcting papers and completed the one she had been working on. She removed her glasses and laid them on her chest, so I quickly looked down at the desk to avoid any misconceptions. She sighed a long, "What a bother" sigh, and asked, "Have we learned anything?" I wanted to say, "How to spell citizen," but I restrained myself and just lied.

"Yes, Mrs. West, I learned not to bother the class and show off."

"Why?"

I searched my mind for just the right answer. I wanted to say, "Because crime doesn't pay," but that sort of sounded like a smart aleck. "I'm not sure," was sure to inspire wrath, so I answered, "The class is here to learn and when I make funny sounds it makes it hard to learn."

"That's a good answer, Gary. I'm assuming that there will not be a next time, but if there is I want you to know that I'm bringing your parents in on it. I wanted to see if we could work it out on our own this time, and I think we have." She leaned over the desk in a threatening way and added, "What do *you* think?"

"I don't think there will be a next time, and I'm glad you

didn't let my parents know." I was sorry later for adding the part about my parents because she sensed that getting my parents involved might prove to be a valuable key in bringing me under control.

"Gary, why do *I* think there *will* be a next time? Don't answer that." She smiled a terribly insincere smile and told me that I could erase the blackboard if I liked. I did erase it as fast as I could and just finished when the bell rang. The class filed in and everyone seemed glad that I was done with my assignment, especially my closest friends. They had been leaderless for nearly four days, but I was back. Bodie hit me in the arm and said, "Way to go, Bud. You did it! Five hundred times, wow! You think that's a record or something?"

"I'm just glad it's over."

"You gonna belch again and crack us all up?"

"I don't think so."

"Why, man?"

"Because Mrs. West said she'd bring my folks into it next time and my dad would kill me for getting in trouble at school. He's got a thing about respecting adults."

"Aren't you going to get old shopping bag eyes for sticking it to you in front of all of us? She made you look like a jerk. No lie," whispered Bodie as we sat down for class.

"Not for a while. I have to be a good C-I-T-I-Z-E-N for a long time."

"I bet that's gonna be real hard for you, huh?"

"Don't know. I never tried it before."

THE REFORMED ME

One day at a time I began to build a new reputation. No, that's really not quite true. Day by day I began to dismantle my old reputation as the class nuisance. I still talked occasionally and had to be shushed, but I complied quickly. My new behavior seemed to mollify Mrs. West's overt hatred of my presence in her class. My buddies were getting singled out now, and I think they kind of missed the old me. I know I did. But with the humiliation of it all still so fresh, I didn't want a new dose to overtake me. And it wouldn't have if I'd just stuck to my new pattern of life.

But one day a messenger entered our room and handed Mrs. West an important note. She read it, and you could tell that she was impressed. It must be really important, I thought, as she rose from her chair. "Class, I must go to the office for a moment. I will be right back. I expect you to behave while I'm gone."

As she slipped out the door the thought occurred to me that the class needed a good laugh. Nearly four weeks had passed since I had been a bad citizen. The class worked quietly as they had been directed and the temptation to belch washed over me like a tidal wave. I felt powerless against the urge, so I issued forth a gastric benevolence the likes of which has not ever been equaled. The class laughed loud and some clapped. I was back. Not that I would do it in Mrs. West's presence, you understand, but it sort of seemed okay to do it when she was out of the room. Or so I thought.

The class calmed down and resumed its study, and I did nothing more to stir it up. Then the door burst open and Mrs. West returned to her desk and sat down. No sooner did she sit down than little Ynez Taggert waved her hand to get Mrs. West's attention. "Yes, Ynez," Mrs. West sweetly inquired.

"While you were out, Gary Richmond belched."

"Thank you, Ynez. Keep working quietly, class," said Mrs. West softly. Then she pulled out a tablet and began to write. Mrs. West wrote and wrote and wrote, three pages of small handwriting recounting everything I had ever done wrong in her class. She signed the finished letter and sealed it in an envelope. Then she smiled at me and asked me to stay after school for just a moment as she had something she wanted me to know.

When the final bell rang, everyone quickly left the room but me. Bodie gave me that "Sorry, friend" look and left with his head down, knowing I was in trouble. I sat nervously while Mrs. West put her desk in order. She didn't seem the least bit in a hurry and seemed to be enjoying making me wait. She even looked up and smiled as she finished up.

"Well, I guess we are ready to go home aren't we, Gary? Here's a little something for you to take with you. Bring it back signed by a parent tomorrow. If you don't have it signed by tomorrow, don't come back until you do have it signed. Do you understand?"

She handed me the document. I could feel the weight of the accusations pull the color of life right out of me. I bet I looked like a ghost. I know I felt like one. I was a walking dead man. When my dad saw the list of things I had done, he was going to spank my bottom shiny, as he used to put it. Then he would yell at me and I would lose a ton of privileges.

"Yes, ma'am," I whispered. Then I lifted my leaden feet and dragged myself across the playground to the school gate. The school principal smiled at me and said, "Hello, son, how are we doing?"

I managed a weak smile and said, "I don't know how *you're* doing, but I don't feel so good. I got to show this letter to my parents, and it's not a very nice letter. Mrs. West is real mad at me for belching, and I got to get a parent to sign it. I'm dead meat."

"Sorry, son. You still have most of the year to get things turned around with Mrs. West. I'd give it my best shot if I were you."

"Yes, sir."

I felt like I was in one of those scenes in an old western movie where the parched miner lifts his canteen to his lips but there isn't any more water in it. He holds it over his head and no water drips out, not one drop, so he throws it with disgust without even bothering to see where it lands. He wipes his arm across his parched and cracked lips and stares at the miles of unforgiving desert that spread out before him. Then he drags one foot at a time toward the horizon, hoping for but not expecting a miracle.

I kept wondering what Mrs. West had said about me. I sort of guessed what the letter might say, and I had to admit that I deserved what I was getting. Then again, maybe it was her fault. All my other teachers knew how to make me mind. Mrs. Warmen, my second grade teacher, was sweet and loving. She hugged me a lot and smiled at me. Being bad for Mrs. Warmen was unthinkable—sort of like spitting on a picture of Joan of Arc. My third grade teacher was firm, fair, and loving. Mrs. Tobin took delight in the success of all of her students. Mr. Yeager was a great teacher who made me love reading and kept me too busy to be bad. Mrs. Bruner was beautiful. I had a terrible crush on her and would do anything to make her smile. She looked and sounded like Snow White. And you could tell she was proud of all of us like we were her own children. Why did I have such a terrible time being good for Mrs. West?

THE LETTER

I walked east on Calaveras Street until it reached a dead end on Maiden Lane, about a half a mile. Then I turned north and walked the last quarter to Mendocino Street The house on the corner belonged to Mr. Shackleford, a successful young lawyer. I kind of wondered if he was the kind of lawyer that defended criminals. I sort of felt like a criminal as I faced the worst part of the journey home, my own driveway. It was a long driveway because our house was set back about one hundred feet from the street.

When I got to the front door I slid the letter under my shirt. I wasn't ready to face the music. I stepped quietly over the threshold and closed the door as softly as I could so as not to disturb my mom. I walked quickly to my room and shoved the letter under my pillow. I wasn't ready to show it to anyone.

I went to the kitchen to get something to eat. Nothing ever bothers my appetite. If anything, eating helped me get through bad things. Besides I might be on bread and water soon. A glass of milk and a bowl of potato chips might make a nice last meal. My mother was where she was every day at this time and most of the time. She was sitting at the kitchen table smoking a cigarette and drinking a glass of wine.

"Hi, Mom."

"Hi. Did you have a good day at school?" That's what my mother always asked, not like she really cared but like that's what she was supposed to say when a kid got home. She didn't look at me but out the window about a million miles from earth, in the world she lived in most of the time. She asked it like it was work to ask it, like she wanted me to say it was fine so she could go back to smoking and drinking and looking out the window.

At least Mom wasn't crying. She did that a lot, but not at the kitchen table. She cried in the bedroom for one or two hours at a time. My dad had told me if it bothered me to just go over to a friend's house till he got home but to leave a note saying where I had gone. My dad had explained that my mother suffered from depression. She was seeing a doctor each week and the doctor was very expensive. Dad had to work almost every weekend to pay the psychiatrist.

Mom wasn't getting better, and my dad was tired all the time, but he didn't complain. He was still an enthusiastic poker player and used to answer many of my questions with poker wisdom. One day I asked him if he wasn't tired of all this stuff. His answer was, "Son, you just play the hand you're dealt. That's all you got so it don't do no good to complain. You just play the game."

Things hadn't always been like that. Everything about my life had been pretty happy until about the middle of my fifth grade year, about the time my mother started suffering from depression. I remembered a time when she had cared about how school had gone. I wanted her to be happy but I didn't know what to do so I didn't think about it much. I just spent more and more time over at friends' houses.

I liked going over to Doug Sigler's the best because he lived with his mom who was a single parent. His dad had run off, and Doug didn't even know where he was. Doug didn't seem to care because he never brought it up too much. Now I realize he probably cared, but it was too painful for him to talk about it. I should have known that then because I never told him that my mother drank too much and cried all the time. Anyway, I liked going over there because we were unsupervised and could get away with murder on a regular basis. Doug's mother worked hard to make ends meet and didn't get home until six every night.

I went back to my room and grabbed the letter and took it to Doug's house. I knocked at the door, hoping he was home. I needed a friend, and he was good one. The door opened and Doug grinned an impish grin. "Man, I didn't think I'd see you for a month after your parents read Mrs. West's letter."

"They haven't seen it yet," I said as I pulled it from beneath my shirt. It was getting a little wrinkled from the way I was carrying it. "Doug, do you think that you can open a letter by steaming it?"

"It works in the movies."

"You got a tea kettle, man?"

"Yeah."

"You suppose we could try steaming this puppy open? I would kind of like to know what it says."

"Won't hurt anything to try," said Doug, his impish grin still intact. He went to the stove where a kettle was already in place with water in it. He turned on the burner full blast. In about four minutes steam was issuing generously from the spout. Doug said, "Let's do it." I held the seam of the envelope over the steam and moved it back and forth for about a minute. Then I pulled it away from the kettle and pulled on the envelope's tab. It came open slick as a whistle.

With trembling fingers I lifted Mrs. West's letter out of the envelope and unfolded it. I knew I was in trouble when I read the first line.

Dear Mr. and Mrs. Richmond,

I must confess that in forty plus years of teaching I have never found myself at a loss in gaining the respect and obedience of a student. But Gary has frustrated all my efforts to bring him under control. I need your help in the worst way and would appreciate any support you can give me.

Gary is a constant distraction to the class and is affecting the learning process of the other twenty-eight children. He talks constantly when I am talking, which makes it difficult to teach. I have asked him repeatedly to stop but to no avail.

Not only does Gary talk incessantly but he has accumulated an arsenal of unusual sounds that he produces during quiet moments intended for study. He belches often and loudly and makes other distasteful sounds, which I will leave to your imagination. They stir the other children up and assault the learning environment to such a degree that I fear that many of our students will not be ready for the seventh grade should we not make headway on bringing your son under control.

I have checked with other teachers who had Gary in their classes and they did not report that these behaviors had yet developed. They have for me, and I beg of you to do all that you can to help me.

Gary rarely works up to his potential because he spends so much of his time and energy disrupting the class. I have asked him repeatedly why he can't be more like his older brother Steve, who as I remember was a delight to have in my class. It seems difficult for me to fathom you have two sons so different. Gary needs to be more like Steve or we will be forced to take more drastic measures than a letter home.

I cannot emphasize enough the gravity of the problems that Gary has brought to our otherwise peaceful class.

Help me please!

Sincerely,
Olivia West

P.S. I have asked Gary to bring me this letter back signed. Thank you in advance for the help you will be to me.

I was staggered. The letter seemed to me an exaggeration. I had no sense that I was being that disruptive. I didn't feel that our class was behind in any way. In fact we had some of the smartest kids in the school. I knew one thing for sure. My parents were going to be on her side. My brother had liked her okay and adults in those days sort of stuck together. I was in trouble and I knew it.

Doug read it over my shoulder and just whistled. Then he said, "Hate to say it, man, but you're in deep grease. Your dad's gonna kill you."

"Thanks for the encouragement, Doug," I sighed. "I got to go. I want to see if my brother will forge my mom's name on the letter. It's my only chance."

I ran home with the letter under my shirt and found my brother outside. Out of breath I said, "You got to help me, Steve. I'm in a lot of trouble and it's partly your fault."

"What do you mean it's partly my fault?" Steve answered indignantly.

"You had to be so good in Mrs. West's class. She keeps saying over and over, 'Why can't you be more like your brother Steve? He was such a good boy. He was quiet and he did his work.' She's mad at me because I'm not like you."

"What did you do to get on her bad side?" asked Steve, who was now curious to see why I was in such a dither.

"I belched a whole bunch of times."

"You what?" he asked as he laughed out loud.

"Well, I made some other noises too."

"What kind of noises?" Steve sounded amused and genuinely interested.

"You know! The opposite of belching!"

"Really!"

"Yeah, really. Now Mrs. West has sent a long letter home that I have to get signed or I can't come back to school. Read the letter." Steve read it out loud and whistled every now and then to show how serious the situation seemed to be.

"You're in deep trouble," he finally said.

"Steve, you got to forge Mom's signature for me. This will

hurt Mom's feelings, and Dad will be so mad he'll kill me."

"I can't do that."

"Why?"

"It's dishonest and besides that, if I got caught I'd be in worse trouble than you're in right now. If I were you, I'd go show Mom right now and get her to sign it. If you get lucky, she'll just mention it to Dad and he won't read it. Maybe he won't kill you if he doesn't actually read it."

FACING THE MUSIC

I was a little suspicious of my brother's advice. He wasn't much of an authority on getting out of trouble because he never got into trouble. Yet his advice did sound like my best chance to retain the spark of life. I took the letter in my hand and walked to the kitchen where nothing had changed. My mother looked up and said, "You're back soon. Dinner's not for an hour and your dad's not home yet."

"I know, Mom. I got to talk to you. It's important."

"Don't you want to talk to your father if it's important?" There was a note of panic in Mom's voice because she didn't like any pressure. She nervously grabbed her cigarettes and lit one, dragging an enormous volume of silky white smoke into her lungs. She held it there and repeated the process again before she asked, "What's so important that it can't wait until your dad gets home?"

"I got into trouble at school, Mom."

"I hope you didn't get into a fight."

"No, Mom, I didn't."

"Thank God for that. Then what did you do?"

"I was kind of a nuisance in class."

"What did you do to get into trouble?"

"I just belched and Mrs. West got real mad. Then she remembered everything I ever did and wrote you a letter about it. She said I had to get you to sign it before I came back to class."

"Let's see the letter." She took the envelope from me and began to read. Big tears began to roll down her cheeks and splash onto the letter. Gee, you'd have thought that Mrs. West had said all those nasty things about *her.* My mother fought back a sob and said, "What kind of a mother must she think that I am? Lord knows I've tried my best, but you're harder than Steve. I never could control you. You're such a disappointment to me." She laid her head on her folded arms and cried while I stood there trying to think of something to say.

"Mom, give me another chance. I'm sorry I let you down. I don't know why I'm bad so much. I don't mean anything by it. I think I can do better and make you proud of me if you'll give me a chance." I was crying now and wishing that I had handed the letter to my dad. He had been in trouble a lot when he was a boy. Even though I'd have gotten a good spanking, by the end of the spanking things would have been even and I could have started all over again fresh. I felt terrible. For the first time I felt like I really was a *bad boy*—the kind that makes his parents ashamed.

"Mom, give me a good punishment. I deserve it," I said sincerely.

"Gary, I don't want your father to find out about this. He's proud of you, and I don't want him to feel terrible. He's tired all the time from working weekends and he doesn't need news like this to break his heart." She took another hit on her wine glass, tossed her hair back, and primped as she regained her composure. She got her Parker fountain pen and signed the letter adding this postscipt:

> I cannot tell you how disappointed Mr. Richmond and I are in Gary's poor behavior. Be assured that we will sup-

port your every effort to bring him into line with your expectations. Should he get out of line in any way, call me at Sycamore 79875. We apologize for the distraction and poor example that Gary has been in class.

> Sincerely,
> Henrietta Richmond

My mother handed the letter back to me and began to cry again. Then she gulped down the rest of her wine and headed for her bedroom. Just before she slammed the door I heard her sob, then say, "I'm a failure as a wife and as a mother. Why can't I do anything right?" I heard her throw herself on the bed, and she spent the next hour crying her heart out.

Man, I wished I had told my dad. It was too late. I knew my brother wasn't an authority on getting in or out of trouble and wondered why I had taken his advice. I would never take his advice on that subject again. I just lay on my bed and listened to my mother crying. I felt I owed her that. I was nervous all evening thinking she might change her mind and tell my dad but she didn't.

BOOKENDS

The next day I handed the letter to Mrs. West and she held my eyes with hers as she opened it. She read my mother's comment and smiled a victory smile. I soon learned that she had orchestrated another surprise for me. Added to the letter, they formed bookends to hold me in place—at least for awhile.

After lunch Mrs. West called the class to order. When the room was quiet, she stood up and said, "Students, our class president, Kenneth Ott, has a presentation to make. Would you all pay attention please?" How aglow she looked. How proud she appeared to be. She liked Kenneth almost as well as she liked little Ynez Taggert and beamed as he made his way to the front of the room. Mrs. West added, "Stand up and come to the front, Gary. The presentation is for you."

I felt sick. Whatever was going to happen couldn't be fun for me. I was sure of that. I could see that Mrs. West was enjoying the moment all too enthusiastically. I reluctantly stepped forward. Kenneth Ott had a little box with a lid. He didn't look me in the eye, but looked down and read a note written on a three by five card. "Gary, since you like to act like a little child, we thought you would like this token of our esteem."

He handed me the box and asked me to open it. Inside was a little toy train, a cheap little plastic job with a shiny black engine, a blue box car, and a brown caboose. I recognized it as a train that had been collected one car at a time from inside cereal boxes—a real thrill for a kid three years old, but a royal put-down for a sixth grader. The demeaning gift was all the more effective coming from my peers. When Kenneth handed it to me, he led the class in applause. About two thirds of the kids applauded but not most of my friends, thank goodness.

That was by far the most humiliating moment of my life. Mrs. West clapped her hands with wild enthusiasm and in a lilting voice chirped, "Well, Gary, don't you want to say something to the class?" I held the train about stomach level as thoughts raced through my mind—none of them good or kind or constructive. I wanted to run from the room and never come back. I wanted to throw the train in Kenneth Ott's face and hit him until I was too tired to hit him anymore. Most of all I wanted to cry, but I didn't. My tears would have proved to everyone that I was a baby and I didn't want to give Mrs. West any more satisfaction than she was experiencing at the moment. I didn't think she could take it without overdosing.

I looked into her eyes and searched them for any sign that she cared how I was feeling at that moment. I found no sign. I pursed my lips defiantly and said nothing as our eyes locked together in a battle of wills. Mrs. West waited. The smile on her face faded but she did not drop her eyes. The class became silent as they felt the tension growing between us.

She broke the silence. "Gary, I asked you a question. Don't you have something you want to say to the class?" The lilt was out of her voice now, and she wasn't enjoying herself anymore. I continued to stare into her eyes and waited till waiting would have drifted into total disrespect. I summoned all of my courage or rebellion or focused anger and said with deep conviction, as I continued to stare into her eyes, "No!"

"No?" Mrs. West said indignantly. "And why not, young man?"

"Because I don't want to get into any more trouble."

"Well, that's good news, but I'll believe it when I see it."

I decided to sit down when she looked away. I wanted to give Kenny Ott a dirty look for being a part of what went on, but he kept looking down. I don't think he really enjoyed the role he had played in my humiliation because we were friends. We would be again when I got through licking my wounds.

After class Bodie asked me if I wanted him to rough up Kenny Ott for what he did, and I said no. Then he asked me if I was going to get back at Mrs. West and I said that I didn't know. I was kind of tired of getting into trouble. The fun that led to the trouble just wasn't worth it anymore. I never did belch in that class again. That was the year I learned I could go too far, that there were boundaries. That was the year I discovered there are always consequences for behavior both good and bad. Sixth grade was one of the most important years of my life. The saga continues in the next chapter.

6

One Can Only Be Good for So Long

DAY FOLLOWED MUNDANE DAY as I behaved myself, much to Mrs. West's amazement. She asked me a few times if I was feeling all right. My having been so good for so long worried her. She thought that I might be ill. Mrs. West said she knew it must be difficult for me to be good for so long and didn't think I could pull it off without the help of being sick. Brother!

Halloween gave way to a chilly California November where temperatures would dip all the way down to the low seventies during the day. Christmas was in the air. You could tell by the weather and also because Mrs. West had brought out her famous Christmas decorations. She handled decorating much like she handled her own facial makeup. She used much too much and didn't improve the appearance a whole lot. Boxes and boxes of decorations were hung. Our room looked like someone had dynamited a toy store. But it was colorful and it did break the monotony.

Mrs. West's pride and joy was nobly displayed eight feet above the floor on a ledge created by the cloak room where we hung our coats and kept our lunches. On top of the divider was Santa and all of his reindeer, led by Rudolph the reindeer mutation. (Perhaps radioactively induced.)

Did I mention I had developed a new ability? The deadly art of shooting spit wads. This sport was then a favorite pastime of sixth grade boys. According to the adults you could put a person's eyes out with a misplaced spit wad. If that was true you could go around school and find a bunch of kids with black patches over their eyes who would say bitterly, "A spit wad did this." But I never met a kid who lost his eye to a spit wad.

Adults typically exaggerate dangers to kids. Mothers especially make everything sound dangerous. Adults just don't want them to get hurt for any reason. Now that I'm an adult, I freely embrace the practice of exaggerating dangers. But unfortunately, these exaggerations lead to a credibility gap. I shot a lot of people and never really hurt anybody with spit wads.

I did find them to be deadly to Christmas displays, however. My spit wad was especially dangerous to Mrs. West's decorations. About eighteen feet from where I sat, Rudolph stood proudly in front of all the rest of the team. Cupid and Comet and Donder and Blitzen and all the rest seemed to be looking to him to guide them, and Santa looked jolly and proud of the whole bunch.

The display was about eight feet in length and mounted on top of generous mounds of cotton that showed all the signs of having been picked during the reconstruction period following the Civil War. You sort of had the feeling the cotton may have had some historic value and that's why Mrs. West kept using it every year. It sure didn't look like snow.

Rudolph's nose especially captured my attention. It was bright red, fire engine red, and it was large. It reminded me of something which eluded me at first, but then it came to me suddenly, in a flash and a twinkle: Rudolph's nose was like the center of every target I had ever seen. It was a bulls-eye that begged to be shot by a spit wad. To hit a target about the size of a quarter from eighteen feet would be quite a coup. No matter how long it took, I would accept the challenge of hitting it.

The greatest challenge was not to get caught doing anything so mischievous. No one knew what Mrs. West would do to me if I got into trouble again, but I was bound and determined to hit that nose once before the display came down in five weeks.

Making a spit wad is an art in itself. You take a piece of paper about four inches by three inches and roll it as tightly as you possibly can. Licking it frequently gives it weight and causes it to stick together. When it is wound as tightly as possible, you bend it in half. It is now a missile, an arrow that will derive its energy and propulsion from a rubber band which is suspended tightly between your thumb and your first finger.

You then mount your V-shaped paper wad over the rubber band, preferably one of the big thick ones you find on the Sunday paper. Holding the ends of the spit wad firmly together in the hand (taking care not to hold the rubber band), you pull it back as far as you can without breaking or snapping the rubber. It's sort of like a poor man's bow and arrow.

When you let go that baby takes a ride. Your only problems are the telltale twang of the rubber band and the noise the spit wad itself makes as it whizzes through the air and hits its target. So you have to shoot it when nobody was looking who would tell on you, and then immediately ditch the rubber band as the only evidence that would connect you to the spit wad.

I really didn't want to get caught so I was very careful as to when I shot my paper wads. Everyone who sat near me was a loyal friend who would never tell a soul about my goal to shoot Rudolph's nose. I had let them in on my plan so they could help me watch out for the students who would enjoy seeing me get into trouble again with Mrs. West.

My first shot should have worried me and even ended my pursuit, but it didn't. I missed Rudolph's nose by a foot but hit Comet in the side. The paper wad rocked Comet enough to almost knock him over. This was not good because all of the reindeer were connected by a little system of reins and if one went over, it was likely to pull down the whole display. But I was focused. I was also entertaining my best friends who were enjoying each shot. Other students were looking around to find the location of the twang, but I had developed a pretty secretive system.

Several days passed and several of the spit wads hung from the cotton just beneath the plastic reindeer. All of them screamed, "Ha, ha, you missed." But the law of averages finally caught up with my experiment. I hit Rudolph right in the nose. I didn't have time to enjoy the moment, however. Rudolph toppled as though he'd been shot by an elephant gun. I watched in disbelief as all nine reindeer, Santa, and his sleigh disappeared from sight and crashed to the floor of the cloak room. It was a horrible sound—the sound of a whole lot of plastic breaking and scattering.

Mrs. West disappeared into the cloak room where she stayed for a long time, saying good-bye to old friends and fond memories. She emerged with fire in her eyes. Out of all the reindeer parts she could have had, she ironically returned with only one: Rudolph's shiny red nose. Mrs. West held it up and rolled it back and forth between her thumb and forefinger and searched the eyes of each student. When she looked at me, I just looked innocent. She kept searching for that set of eyes that would betray the perpetrator so that she could exact her punishment. No one but Bodie Hull had seen me shoot, and he would die before betraying me. I was home free. Or so I thought.

NO ESCAPE

At last Mrs. West spoke. "That display has presided over Christmas for the last fifteen years. It was a gift intended to bring pleasure to the students in my class. I hope someone is satisfied with how you have hurt me. It's as simple as this. Until the person who has done this comes forward, the rest of the class will not be allowed to leave the room for any reason during the coming days. You can either show courage and come forward, or those of you who know can tell me who did this so that the whole class is not unfairly punished for the dastardly deed of one selfish individual."

Mrs. West then sat down in her chair still fingering Rudolph's nose. My great grandmother would have described her as madder than a wet hen.

The class sat in stunned silence, hoping that the offender would come forth and take the wrath that person alone deserved. The recess bell rang, and I stood up. I spoke respectfully. "Mrs. West, there is no need to punish the class for what I did."

She looked stunned. "Class dismissed. Gary, you stay here." The class filed out, thankful for my honesty. I sat down and awaited the unabated wrath of Mrs. West to blow over me like a nuclear wind. I fully expected to be ashes and rubble within seconds. I was truly ashamed and embarrassed, maybe for the first time. I just stared at the floor waiting for the pendulum to swing or the axe to fall.

When it didn't, I looked up to find Mrs. West looking at me—not in a mean or angry way, but as if she were calling on her forty years of teaching experience to make some sense of this moment. She looked tired, hurt, and confused, but she didn't look angry.

I broke the silence. "I haven't been a good citizen in the past, Mrs. West, but I had been trying lately to be better. I don't know if you'll believe me, but I wasn't trying to knock the display down, just hit it with a spit wad. In fact, all I was trying to hit was Rudolph's nose." Mrs. West rolled her eyes and held up Rudolph's nose and looked at it.

"When I did I was going to stop trying anymore. I got carried away. I know how much you loved your reindeer display. I don't know how much it cost you to buy it, but I have saved up about fifteen dollars and if it's more I will earn it up and give the rest to you as I get the money. What I want you to believe—I know it will be hard—is that I didn't mean to hurt your feelings or knock down the reindeer display. I'm very sorry, and I deserve whatever punishment you decide to give me."

Mrs. West set the nose down and put her hands together in a praying position and closed her eyes. She was silent for about twenty seconds. "Gary, I believe you, and I appreciate your sincere offer to replace the display. It was a gift. I wouldn't know what to charge. I will retire in two years so getting another one wouldn't be timely. I will attempt to glue this one together. From a distance... well, that leaves me with what to do about today. Nothing I have done to you has proven totally effective, so I'm asking you what *you* would do to you? What would you do to a boy like you that would put a stop to his going too far?"

I thought hard. That was a pretty tough question because I was a handful. I could see Mrs. West smile just for a second when she saw that I was taking her assignment seriously.

"I've always been afraid that you'd make me wear the dunce cap. You always said you might do that, and no kid like me likes to look stupid in front of his friends. I've always wondered why you haven't tried that on me because I would hate it fiercely."

Mrs. West looked very surprised that I would admit my fear of that punishment. I was just as surprised that she hadn't gotten to know me well enough to know that the dunce cap was the worst thing she could do to me. Mrs. West rose from her chair, went into the cloak closet, and returned with the dreaded cap.

"You know, nobody has worn this for a while, and it used to be considered a pretty effective weapon against poor classroom deportment. Gary Richmond, I'll do anything necessary to make you mind, although I have grown weary of the task. Yet still, it is mine and I will not hand it to another. Get that stool over there and take it to the corner in the front of the classroom." I did as I was told. "Now sit on that stool and face the class." I sat on the stool and she carefully placed the dunce cap on my head. "Stay on the stool till lunch."

Meanwhile, Mrs. West carefully gathered the broken display pieces and put them into a shopping bag. When the class filed in they got a pretty good laugh, but it didn't bother me like I thought it would, because I deserved my punishment. I kind of felt like the good thief on the cross must have felt. Two days later, Santa and his reindeer had been glued together and returned to their lofty place. From a distance it didn't really look so bad. I felt a little better.

THE COLD WAR

I would like to say that incident ended all the hard feelings and cured my tendency to be a bad citizen, but I cannot. Mrs. West must have had new hope of reforming me. With renewed vigor she set out to see if humiliation would some-how bring me into submission. It only made me angry. So the cold war escalated. I continued providing nuisance value, and she continued striking back with belittling remarks and degrading punishments. I didn't like her, and she didn't like me. I was a gnat in her ear and she was a fly swatter.

That year was probably the hardest year of our educational lives and the most memorable for all the wrong reasons. I was never caught again for anything serious. The last thing worthy of punishment that I did was to accept a dare from Bodie Hull and Doug Sigler.

"We dare you to put a tack on Mrs. West's chair. We double and *triple* dare you to put a tack on Mrs. West's chair. What comes after triple dare?" asked Bodie.

"Quadruple dare," I answered smugly.

"We do that too!" added Doug.

I'd never been quadruple dared before and there seemed to be something solemn about it. No self-respecting class comic, bad citizen, pugnacious, rambunctious rounder could possibly walk away from a quadruple dare. "What'll I get if I do it?"

Bodie chimed in, "We'll take you to Kern's Delicatessen for a kosher dill pickle, a Dad's Old Fashioned Root Beer, a slice of his world famous pumpernickel bread, and a piece of Swiss cheese." Doug stared at Bodie who was from a rich family and said, "Before you go making plans for *my* money, you better ask me first. If you knew Gary better, you'd know he'd have done it for *free.*"

"Not anymore," I quickly added.

"Then I'm good for it, Doug. You don't even have to kick in anything," said Bodie with conviction. He stuck out his hand and we shook on it. I could already taste the tangy pickle and imagine it snapping crisply as I bit into it with my usual gusto. Mrs. West had a date with a tack.

The next day we were playing kickball during recess. I was playing right field and the other team was up with no outs. Mrs. West seemed to be fairly absorbed in a conversation with Mrs. Bruner, the fifth grade teacher. I kept slowly backing up until I was near the boys' bathroom, and when I thought she wasn't looking slipped inside. I peered at Mrs. West from around the corner of the door. The coast seemed to be clear.

I backed into the hallway and ran to the end to the stairs that led down one floor below our room, then ran down the stairs very careful not to let even one person see me. Once outside the school, I ran west and reentered the building downstairs just below my own classroom. I ran back up the stairs and peeked around the corner to see if anyone was standing in our hallway. No one in sight. My plan was working beautifully.

I ran into our room and placed a tack slightly to the right near the back of Mrs. West's seat. Then I quietly slipped out of the room and backtracked my route until I was again standing in the boys room. Mrs. West and Mrs. Bruner were still talking and as far as I knew. No one saw me leave or return. I just slipped back into the game, and found there were now two outs. When the third out was made I stood near Mrs. West to make sure she saw me outside with the rest of the kids.

When the bell rang ending recess, I walked just in front of her and chatted a little to make sure she could account for my whereabouts at all times. She watched me go right to my desk and pull out my books. Mrs. West remained standing for a long period following the recess because her next lesson was at the board. Bodie and Doug knew I had made my move. They also knew that the shiny tack was sitting like a rattlesnake ready to nail her as soon as she sat down.

All of our sinister little hearts were pounding as we waited for those fateful words, "Now class, take out a piece of paper and write a sentence using each of the ten words we have just learned." Mrs. West closed her spelling book and moved around to her chair. Just before sitting, she pulled up her silky dress to give her legs more freedom. Then she sat.

This is where Mrs. West should have reacted swiftly and dramatically—but she didn't. She didn't flinch, wince, jerk, or jump, nor in any of the usual ways associated with sitting on a tack. Doug and Bodie and I exchanged quick glances indicating our confusion. We were all saying, "How can this be?" with our eyes.

But there she sat, her head down and deep in concentration. I had underestimated my teacher. The normal person could not concentrate while sitting on a tack. My mind raced for an explanation.

1. Maybe the tack fell on the floor when she pulled the chair out to sit down.
2. Maybe her nerves were shot where she sat down and she didn't have the normal feelings younger people experience when they sit on a tack.
3. Maybe she flat crushed the little sucker when she sat down.
4. Maybe she's sitting there in severe pain but will not give any of us the satisfaction of knowing it. Maybe after we have left the room for lunch, she will screech and remove the tack when we won't see it.

The amazing mystery would soon be solved when Mrs. West finally stood up and walked from behind her desk. She didn't notice that her dress was hanging funny and her slip was showing. When she turned around, we discovered that Mrs. West had sat on the tack right where she was supposed to have sat on the tack. Her dress even looked worse in the back because about six inches of her slip was revealed. The tack—shiny and clearly visible for all the world to see—was holding her dress up.

Why Mrs. West was feeling no pain was still a bit of a mystery, but evidently the tack pierced her dress, slip, and girdle and just didn't have enough tip left to penetrate her skin. It must have felt scratchy because she kept rubbing where the tack was. Of course Doug and Bodie and I were experiencing a male-bonding moment. It was everything we could do to keep from laughing hysterically. We didn't for fear that when she sat down again, the point would finally be driven home. None of us could afford to get into trouble.

Finally Mrs. West noticed that her slip was very revealed. She yanked her dress down, dislodging the tack and sending it sailing down the middle row of the classroom. She heard it but did not see it and never discovered that she had been had.

Bodie made good on his offer and I savored every bite of the delicacies I had so learned to love. Life hardly gets better than when a sixth grade boy comes through on a dare and is rewarded in such a kingly manner. Life was grand.

THE RECITATION

Life got one notch better and I am happy to report that my sixth-grade year ended on a happy note for me. In some ways it was a victory for both Mrs. West and me.

Once a quarter we were given the option to memorize a poem or recitation of our choice as approved by Mrs. West. The first three quarters I chose relatively short, usually humorous little offerings best described as just enough to meet the minimum expectation. I did not wish to excel in her class for fear of giving Mrs. West the satisfaction that something she had done had inspired me. The last quarter of the year had arrived and it was again time to choose our selection.

One day in early April Mrs. West asked with just a note of sarcasm and a pinch of disdain, "So what are we thinking about choosing for the recitation this time, Gary? Something short and filled with mirth no doubt." She smiled that condescending, you're-poor-white-trash-compared-to-your-brother smile of hers, and I could feel my face flush with anger.

I didn't let a second pass before I tossed out, "I've been thinking of a Robert W. Service poem from his collection entitled *The Spell of the Yukon.*"

"I'm familiar with that work. Which poem did you think was short enough to memorize?"

"Well, I can't make up my mind between 'The Shooting of Dan Magrew' or 'The Cremation of Sam McGee,'" I quickly countered.

"Gary, both of those poems are at least four pages long. Nobody in my class has ever even attempted to memorize four pages, not even the better students. Why don't you be realistic and bite off no more than you can chew?"

"I could do it if I wanted to."

"Gary, you have never wanted to do very much before, and I just think you're talking big to show off. I'll just be pleased if you pick another short funny piece like you usually do with no more talk about a four-page poem."

"What if that's the one I want to choose?"

"Gary, you do continue to make things difficult. I would have to get a note from your parents saying they know your choice and will help you with it."

"I'll bring you the note tomorrow."

Why did I do that? I didn't like to memorize poems. The weather was warming up. It was time for bare feet and baseball. It was time for hiking and going to Devil's Gate Dam to hunt snakes and frogs. It was time to wash schoolwork out of your hair and get ready for summer vacation. Just the sound of those two carefree, wonderfully irresponsible words! SUMMER VACATION!

Memorizing four pages could take a lot of free time, play time, discretionary time. I wondered how long each page would take to memorize. I had two months. I took out a book and looked at a page and gasped. It was longer than the Pledge of Allegiance and the Declaration of Independence put together. If I continued with this folly, it would be like going to prison for a long time. All I would have was the satisfaction of wiping that terrible, demeaning smile off of her face.

That settled it. I'd do it.

That night when my dad got home, I asked him if he would write a note saying he would help me memorize one of Robert W. Services' epic poems. He asked, "Son, why'd you pick these poems?"

"Two reasons, Dad. Mrs. West doesn't think I'm smart enough to remember them. She doesn't think I have what it takes, and I want to prove she's wrong. I like these poems. You've read them to me since I was old enough to understand them."

"Your reasons are good enough, son. I'll stand with you on this one. For what it's worth, I believe you can do it." Dad squeezed my shoulder and grabbed a fountain pen and a piece of paper and wrote simply:

Dear Mrs. West,

Gary has our approval to memorize a poem from Robert W. Service's *Spell of the Yukon*. We will work with him as he seeks to accomplish his goal.

Respectfully,
Walter E. Richmond

My dad handed me the note and pulled down his favorite book of poems from our bookshelf. He looked at it for a moment, holding it with his strong hands, rough enough to plane a door. The book was filled with poems about men like him. Dad was not the academic type, too anemic a word for him. He was good and kind and reliable, strong like John Henry and wise in the ways of the world. He was nobody's sucker bait. He was a good husband and a great father. If his life had been different, my dad could have been anything he would have wanted to be. But he didn't complain. He wasn't that kind of man.

I took the book to my room and read both "The Shooting of Dan Magrew" and "The Cremation of Sam McGee" out loud. I loved them both, but in the end a poem about a man who freezes to death looking for gold in the Yukon and makes his friend promise to cremate him if he dies captured my imagination. My choice would be "The Cremation of Sam McGee."

The next day I handed the note to Mrs. West and waited for her to open it and see my father's support. She read it and smirked, then shook her head and turned to me. "Are you sure you want to do this? It would be better to succeed at an easier task than fail a large one."

"I don't plan to fail," I answered. "I also expect an A when I succeed."

"You'll get your A, but you'll have to do it well." I was dismissed. The conversation was over. All that remained was to do it.

Have you ever tried to memorize a four-page poem? If you have, you'll know what my next two months were like. I fell asleep many nights during the next eight weeks with that open book in my bed. I woke up many mornings to find the book was my pillow. The poem was so long that I found it hard not to forget the beginning as I was working on the end.

Yet as the days went by I found the drive I needed to keep on keeping on when Mrs. West would continue to encourage me to give it up. Three days before my turn to recite, I still had not been able to accomplish the four pages without being cued three or four times. That wasn't good enough. Every spare moment was spent repeating the phrases I found most difficult. The night before, my dad—as he had every night—listened as I poured out all I had remembered. I finally got through with only one reminder.

My dad was proud. He knew he had been the inspiration for the poem that I had chosen, that I had chosen it out of my respect for him. I never said how much I loved and re-spected him, but Dad knew it—just like he never told me that he loved me, but I knew it through his every action.

"You're ready, son. She's gonna have to give you that A, and if she doesn't I'll be down there to find out why. You've done really good and I'm proud, really proud."

When class opened the next morning I was as nervous as a long-tailed cat in a room full of rocking chairs. I stumbled over the flag salute. Oh brother, was this going to be a disaster, I thought. At least five students went before me that morning and all did very well, certainly well enough to add to my anxiety. I hadn't taken into account what I would feel like in front of my friends and the other kids in the class.

Finally the moment of truth came, the moment of testing. I walked from my desk to the front of the class. It was about a mile, I think.

Mrs. West said, "Class, Gary has picked a very long selec-tion from a collection of poems that capture the spirit of the Alaskan gold rush. You will no doubt find it entertaining, if Gary can remember it. It's very long, and no one has ever done a poem this long before in my class."

I just wasn't sure why she had to say all that just before I went on, but it had a good effect on me. Her comments gave me an industrial strength dose of, "I'll show you!" When she stopped talking, I stood tall and found my voice.

The Cremation of Sam McGee

There are strange things done in the midnight sun
  By the men who moil for gold;
The Arctic trails have their secret tales
  That would make your blood run cold;
The Northern Lights have seen queer sights,
  But the queerest they ever did see
Was that night on the marge of Lake Lebarge
  I cremated Sam McGee.

Now Sam McGee was from Tennessee, where the cotton
  blooms and blows.
Why he left his home in the South to roam 'round the
  Pole, God only knows.
He was always cold, but the land of gold seemed to hold
  him like a spell;
Though he'd often say in his homely way that he'd sooner
  live in hell.

On a Christmas Day we were mushing our way over the
  Dawson Trail.
Talk of you're cold! through the parka's fold it stabbed
  like a driven nail.
If our eyes we'd close, then the lashes froze till sometimes
  we couldn't see;
It wasn't much fun, but the only one to whimper was Sam
  McGee.

And that very night, as we lay packed tight in our robes beneath the snow,
And the dogs were fed, and the stars o'erhead were dancing head and toe,
He turned to me, and "Cap," says he, "I'll cash in this trip, I guess;
And if I do, I'm asking that you won't refuse my last request."

Well, he seemed so low that I couldn't say no; then he says with a sort of moan:
"It's the cursed cold, and it's got right hold till I'm chilled clean through to the bone.
Yet t'ain't being dead—it's my awful dread of the icy grave that pains;
So I want you to swear that, foul or fair, you'll cremate my last remains."

A pal's last need is a thing to heed, so I swore I would not fail;
And we started on at the streak of dawn; but God! he looked ghastly pale.
He crouched on the sleigh, and he raved all day of his home in Tennessee;
And before nightfall a corpse was all that was left of Sam McGee.

There wasn't a breath in that land of death, and I hurried, horror-driven,
With a corpse half hid that I couldn't get rid, because of a promise given;
It was lashed to the sleigh, and it seemed to say: "You may tax your brawn and brains,
But you promised true, and it's up to you to cremate those last remains."

Now a promise made is a debt unpaid, and the trail has its
own stern code.
In the days to come, though my lips were dumb in my
heart how I cursed that load.

In the long, long night, by the lone firelight, while the
huskies, round in a ring,
Howled out their woes to the homeless snows—O God!
How I loathed the thing.

And every day that quiet clay seemed to heavy and heavier
grow;
And on I went, though the dogs were spent and the grub
was getting low;
The trail was bad, and I felt half mad, but I swore I would
not give in;
And I'd often sing to the hateful thing, and it hearkened
with a grin.

Till I came to the marge of Lake Lebarge, and a derelict
there lay;
It was jammed in the ice, but I saw in a trice it was called
the "Alice May."
And I looked at it, and I thought a bit, and I looked at my
frozen chum;
Then "Here," said I, with a sudden cry, "is my cre-ma-tor-
ium."

Some planks I tore from the cabin floor, and I lit the boiler
fire;
Some coal I found that was lying around, and I heaped the
fuel higher;
The flames just soared, and the furnace roared—such a
blaze you seldom see;

And I burrowed a hole in the glowing coal, and I stuffed in
Sam McGee.

Then I made a hike, for I didn't like to hear him sizzle so;
And the heavens scowled, and the huskies howled, and the
wind began to blow.
It was icy cold, but the hot sweat rolled down my cheeks,
and I don't know why;
And the greasy smoke in an inky cloak went streaking
down the sky.

I do not know how long in the snow I wrestled with grisly
fear;
But the stars came out and they danced about 'ere again I
ventured near;
I was sick with dread, but I bravely said: "I'll just take a
peep inside.
I guess he's cooked, and it's time I looked;..." then the
door I opened wide.

And there sat Sam, looking cool and calm, in the heart of
the furnace roar;
And he wore a smile you could see a mile, and he said:
"Please close that door.
It's fine in here, but I greatly fear you'll let in the cold and
storm—
Since I left Plumtree, down in Tennessee, it's the first time
I've been warm."

There are strange things done in the midnight sun
By the men who moil for gold;
The Arctic trails have their secret tales
That would make your blood run cold;
The Northern Lights have seen queer sights,

But the queerest they ever did see
Was that night on the marge of Lake Lebarge
I cremated Sam McGee.

I was on a roll. Line followed line, stanza followed stanza. I could see that the class was struck by the sheer immensity of the task I had accomplished. By the end of the second page, the class was leaning forward interested in the tragic circumstances of Sam and Cap. They listened as Sam died and poor Cap mushed through blinding snow and fought his way to the furnace in which he had promised to cremate the frozen corpse of Sam McGee.

On the forth page I faltered and hesitated for a second. Mrs. West, having been captured by my effort, slipped me the word quietly, and I raced to the conclusion where Cap starts the fire and puts Sam's body in the furnace only to watch him sit up and say, "Since I left Plumbtree, down in Tennessee, it's the first time I've been warm."

When I finished, the class went wild cheering and laughing. They liked the ending and they liked it that the class underdog pulled one out. Even Mrs. West was excited for me and really said some very nice things to me later—none of them laced with the sarcasm I had come to expect. That was one of the best days of my life, one of my fondest memories.

Do you know why? I had discovered my potential. It would have taken something like that for me ever to have discovered that I could accomplish something that pushed my brains to their limits.

WHO'S TO BLAME?

Let me briefly tie as many loose ends together as I can. Mrs. West retired two years later to Pasadena. My brother saw her frequently for a few years while he worked at the Pantry

Food Market. She always asked about me. Her favorite question with a twinkle in her eye was, "Is your brother Gary in jail yet?" When Steve told her I was in ministry, she just shook her head as I sometimes do when I remember those days when I worked so hard at not being a good citizen.

I really cannot explain why I was as bad as I was in sixth grade. Oh, I bet some junior psychologists would say, "Easy call." A twelve-year-old boy's mother was dysfunctional, neurotic, and alcoholic. His father was working a lot to pay the medical bills and he lacked the kind of attention that would have offered him the necessary guidance to help him react properly to his environment. It was his mother's fault.

But was it? My mother's father was killed during the First World War, and she was raised by a stepfather who was either very mean to her or neglectful. He was an alcoholic who cheated on her mother every time he got a chance. So it must have all started with my step-grandfather. But maybe not. He had had a mean father and then was orphaned. He didn't even know his birthday. I bet it went that way all the way back to Adam.

So who is to blame? Maybe it was my friends. They were forever prodding me on to new depths of degradation. They dared me so many times I lost count. Their reactions always inspired me to do more bad things just for the attention. Was I just powerless against the pressure of my peers?

Maybe Mrs. West inspired my bad behavior. Perhaps it was her favoritism of other students, her lack of sensitivity to my home life, her provocative negative approach. Yet she couldn't have been all bad. Mrs. West helped me discover my potential—not the way I would have chosen, but somehow it worked and I'm thankful. And I have no idea what influences were at work in her life.

No, it was none of the above. Not really. It was me. I was to blame for my own inexcusable behavior—behavior I would never tolerate from my own son or anyone else's.

I am saddened that our present age seems fixed on the idea that the majority of our behavior can be laid at our parents' doorstep or gravestone. Such a conclusion makes it more difficult to obey the only commandment that has a happiness clause: "Honor your father and your mother that your days may be long on the earth that the Lord your God has given you" (Ex 20:12). The Hebrew word translated "long" means as full or packed with good things as possible. It would be our word for happiness.

Certainly extreme victimization occurs. We will all be judged fairly before God. Mercy, love, and grace will abound where appropriate. But we will have to give account for our choices, including whether we chose to ask God's help to overcome the abuses we've all endured and the bad influences that have always tugged and pulled at our very being.

When I look back at these days thirty-six years ago, I laugh at myself and pray none of my children will ever treat a teacher as I did. Both of my daughters are teaching and I pray that they will never have a student like I was for Mrs. West. The truth is, at age eleven I knew right from wrong. In each of these instances, I chose to do wrong. Had my patterns continued much longer, Mrs. West's question about whether or not I was in jail yet would have been more prophetic than humorous.

Here I am forty-seven years old and as convinced as anyone can be that I am responsible for everything I do and will be held responsible for my choices for good or for evil. I have no desire to blame anyone for anything anymore. It wouldn't do me any good, and it wouldn't make things better. I'm choosing to get well from the effects of being human. The rehabilitation is a lifetime process. Jump in! The water's fine.

7

You Can't Be Too Careful

I'VE ALWAYS LOVED BOOKS AND WRITING, the best of the gifts given to me by my mother. The library was my second home by the time I was six years old. By ten I had checked out every book they had on dinosaurs, the sea and its creatures, especially sharks. Then I turned to land animals—snakes and lizards were my favorites—and then on to animal stories.

By eleven I had discovered mystery novels, or "whodunnits" as my dad called them. I think I read all of the Perry Mason stories. By twelve I couldn't get enough of science fiction and horror. I'm not sure why I liked scaring myself intentionally. Many was the night I would go to sleep with my covers over my head so that I wouldn't see aliens, vampires, werewolves, ghouls, and demons staring at me through my bedroom window.

None of these books affected me more than Neville Schute's *On the Beach*, a well-written story about the world coming to an end because of global nuclear war. As I remember the plot, the United States and Russia go to war and then everyone that can jumps in. Radiation from all the bombs begins to spread out slowly and eventually covers the whole earth.

As it turns out, the inhabitants of Australia have a few weeks longer to live before the nuclear fallout reaches them. They have not been involved in the war and are at a lower latitude than most civilized countries. Since everyone knows they are going to die very soon, they do things they would never have done had they been looking forward to a normal life span—like driving race cars insanely fast and taking incredible chances.

One nuclear submarine still seems to be operational. Someone decides that they should journey to the United States and see if anyone or anything is surviving. One of the best parts of the book is when the sub surfaces in San Francisco Bay. The city is intact, but everyone is dead. The scene is eerie and final, and, it left me absolutely terrified.

Shute dwells a lot on the effects of massive doses of radiation, graphically listing all the symptoms of radiation sickness. The idea of unseen rays destroying your body without anything that could be done to help was horrifying. The thought of your hair falling out, nausea, weakness, and watching all your friends dropping all around you like flies was almost too much to bear.

The creepiest part is when the Australian government passes out these little red cyanide pills. You take them or give them to your loved ones if you are beginning to suffer the hopeless effects of lethal radiation. The low point telling of a young family who ends it all leads you to total despair. In the end nothing remains but rabbits, with a good chance they will all soon die. The story tells of total annihilation of all living things on the earth.

I read that book in two days. I was home with a mild flu bug, but not so sick that I couldn't read. One of the reasons the book scared the wits out of me was that my flu symptoms were identical to the early signs of radiation sickness! I quickly became convinced that I might be suffering from a grand dose of radiation. Nuclear weapons were being tested in Nevada at the time, and for all I knew the whole town of Altadena, California, was the innocent victim of radioactive fallout. I could have been dying and not even know it. Oh, the terrible injustice of it all.

A MATTER OF SURVIVAL

As I closed the book, I resolved to do everything in my power to survive a world gone mad with weapons that could wipe us all out in a matter of days. What to do? Building a bomb shelter struck me as a reasonable initial step, so I planned to begin construction in our backyard as soon as I got well.

I had a rich friend at Elliot Junior High School whose parents had built a bomb shelter in their backyard. At the time I thought a bomb shelter was a little stupid. But after reading *On the Beach*, I decided the Farnsworths were the most astute family in Altadena. Without his parent's permission, Eddie took me down into it. I would pattern my shelter after theirs, with two sets of bunk beds and storage sections in the walls for food and water. They had also neatly stored blankets, medical supplies, and clothing in the shelter. Every ounce of space was used for something important. Eddie said they even had guns down there to keep anyone else out.

One problem remained. You can't just build a bomb shelter without your parents' permission, so I approached my father carefully. Our lives perhaps depended on my presentation. I had made a drawing showing the dimensions of the shelter and was very prepared to justify its need.

"Dad, do you think we could talk?"

"Something wrong?"

"No. Well, yes."

"Are you in trouble again?"

"No, Dad. But I think we all could be if we're not careful."

"You didn't get the neighbors mad at us again, did you?"

"No, Dad."

"What kind of trouble could we all be in, son?"

"Nuclear war."

"Nuclear war?"

"I just read a book about nuclear war, and it's real possible for us to have one."

"There isn't going to be a nuclear war, son."

"Mr. Farnsworth's a doctor and he had an expensive bomb shelter built in back of his garage in case of a nuclear war. He's a very intelligent man, Dad. Maybe he knows something we don't."

"So if a war starts why don't you go over to Eddie's house and get in his bomb shelter?"

"They got guns, Dad. They're just planning on saving their family. That's why I wanted to talk to you. I want to build a bomb shelter in *our* backyard."

"You what?"

I spread out my plans on the kitchen table and Dad studied them while he sipped his steaming cup of coffee. A smile spread over his face as he said, "Looks pretty good to me, Gary. How much you figure it will cost?"

"I'm not sure. But I wanted to use the scrap lumber in back of the garage to shore up the side of the hole I want to dig."

"Yeah, you'll need the lumber. Your hole is ten-by-ten and eight feet deep. You going to dig the hole, son?"

"Yeah, Dad. I know you work real hard so I thought I would do the hole myself."

"You going to get your friends to help?"

"I don't think I better."

"Why?"

"They might figure they could get in the shelter if a war breaks out. There's not going to be room for anybody but our family. It will even be crowded for us. But it's better than getting fried and dying of radiation sickness. Dad, radiation sickness makes you puke your guts up and your hair fall out. Then you get weaker and weaker until you die. It's the pits."

"Show me where you're going to dig the hole, son." I was getting excited. I didn't think he'd go for it. We went out behind our garage and I showed him where I had staked out the dimensions of the shelter.

"Where are you going to put the extra dirt?" All we had in our backyard was grass with a four-foot strip of bare ground around it. That's where I thought the dirt could go. It would give a little landscaped look to the yard.

My dad agreed to let me begin to dig—on the condition that everything be returned to normal if I abandoned the project, which my father said he expected me to do not too long after I started digging the hole. I was thrilled, and my father was amused. He returned to the house to tell my mother what I was going to do. He had a you-gotta-be-kidding smile all over his face and I knew he wasn't taking this nuclear stuff very seriously. But how would he feel when our family was the only family in the neighborhood to survive a first strike? Pretty proud of his thirteen-year-old son, that's how.

I grabbed a point-nosed shovel and started digging. I decided to start with a six-by-six hole eight feet deep. If things stayed cool with the Russians, I would enlarge it to ten-by-ten. A family of four wouldn't have much room in the six-by-six shelter with all the supplies, but it would sure beat being nuked.

I worked most of Saturday. The deeper I dug the harder the ground became. I added a pick to my construction equipment and continued to make slow but steady progress. By the end of the day, the six-foot square hole was nearly three feet deep. I could not believe how much dirt that sucker held. I was bone tired Saturday night and soaked in hot water for nearly an hour. I flopped into bed at 8:00 p.m. and was asleep like a rock in two minutes.

I was out digging again by 8:00 the next morning and determined to make steady progress. But the lower I dug, the more difficult the job became. On Sunday I was able to deepen the hole only a foot and a half more. Still, it looked impressive. I worked every afternoon after school until it was dark, making a foot a day before having to stop for dinner.

By the afternoon of the fourth day, the hole was six feet deep. I was descending by way of a step ladder when I heard the graveled voice of Violet Granthom, our ancient next-door neighbor. She was in her late eighties. "What in heaven's name do you think you're doing, young man?"

"I'm building a bomb shelter in case of a nuclear attack," I said proudly.

"You sure that's not a grave? It looks like a grave to me," she said with a note of suspicion in her voice. She squinted and studied the impressive hole. Her eyes got big as saucers as she continued, "I listen to the news every night on channel four. Haven't heard a stitch about war. I don't care much for the Russkies and don't think they have the grit to tackle the red, white, and blue. I don't think that's a bomb shelter. Looks like a grave." Mrs. Granthom searched my face for a clue as to what I was really doing.

"No, Mrs. Granthom. It's a bomb shelter and it's just for our family."

"You mean if an atomic war did start, you'd turn helpless

people away? Are you saying if I came over and said, 'Please, please, I don't want to die, please don't let me die,' you'd turn me out?"

"I wouldn't want to, Mrs. Granthom, but I'm just building it for our family. Maybe you could have one built on your property for you and your family."

"I can't afford one of those things. What do they cost?"

"I'm just using scrap lumber. I can't afford a fancy one like my friend Eddie Farnsworth. His dad's a doctor. Their bomb shelter is made out of concrete and steel and has air vents and stuff like that. They even got guns to keep people out."

Mrs. Granthom sighed and watched me crawl down into the hole and begin to shovel dirt out. She called down to me, "How deep is it?" I answered, "Six feet, Mrs. Granthom."

"Same depth as a grave. I find that coincidental," she said with renewed suspicion. "You been holding a grudge against anybody, son?"

"Mrs. Granthom, it's really a bomb shelter. You'll see."

MY DAD'S BARGAIN

I continued to dig for the next three days until at last my hole was six feet by six feet wide and eight feet deep. I cut the scrap lumber with a hand saw and made braces to shore up the sides. It looked reminiscent of an old mine shaft. At least the sides wouldn't cave in on us now. I wasn't at all sure what kind of top the bomb shelter should have, but I was sure that my dad would have some suggestions when he got home from work. I knew it would need to be lined with lead to prevent radiation from penetrating and killing us before we knew we were being fried.

When my dad got home he joined me by the shelter. He

nodded his head and said, "Well, Gary you did it. You moved a lot of earth—more than I thought you would. I'm proud of you. How can I help you?"

"Dad, it needs a top. It has to be heavy enough so it won't blow off during the blast. And it's got to let air in so we can breathe. Do you have any suggestions?"

"You're asking the wrong man. You need someone that works with iron and steel."

"What would something like that cost, Dad?"

"It would have to be custom made. Maybe two hundred dollars or more."

"Wow! That stuff's expensive."

"Construction material doesn't come cheap."

"Would you and Mom like to help?"

"This is your project. Like I said, I don't think we're going to have a big war with Russia, at least not for a long time. Whatever you make is going to have to be made out of scrap."

"But, Dad, scrap would probably blow apart."

"Gary, I think you're right."

"Dad, did I just waste a ton of time for nothing?"

"Maybe not. I have a proposition to make. That's a big hole. It would hold a lot of stuff. The garage is full of junk I've been wanting to throw away for a long time. There is a pile of leaves by the side of the house that needs hauling to the dump. We have a lot more scrap lumber that's breeding termites by the side of the garage. Your mother probably has some stuff she'd like tossed out. I'd have to rent a trailer and haul it away, but we could forget the trailer and throw it in your hole there. I'll give you twenty-five dollars if we can use your hole for that purpose. What do you say?"

Well, that was a pile of money in 1957 and there was no way I could afford a two-hundred-dollar custom bomb shelter top. It wasn't what I had in mind, but it didn't take a genius to figure out what would happen if I said no. I'd have to fill up the hole for nothing. I put out my hand, and my dad and I shook on it. No lawyer in the world ever made a more binding contract. When you shook hands with my father it was good as gold, money in the bank.

There isn't a whole lot more to tell. You couldn't believe how much junk we threw into that hole. Unbelievable! After we tossed the last piece of old plumbing in, we filled the hole in with leaves. I jumped up and down on the leaves and when they wouldn't pack down any more I began to shovel in loose dirt and jump up and down on it some more. Then I would water it, throw in more dirt, and jump up and down again. My dad said to make a mound over the hole because the dirt would settle in time, and so I did.

I was putting the finishing touches on the mound, raking it smooth, jumping up and down and raking some more. My back was to the fence when I heard the grave voice of old Mrs. Granthom. "Was a grave, wasn't it, boy?"

I jumped a mile when she spoke. I had been deep in thought about how to spend my earnings. Money has always burned a hole in my pocket.

She giggled and said, "You jumped like a man with a guilty conscience. Now 'fess up. What's in that grave?"

"Nothing's in the grave. It's not a grave," I answered with an exasperated voice.

"Why'd you call it a grave then?" she said like she had me.

"Because you called it a grave, Mrs. Granthom. It was going to be a bomb shelter, but I couldn't afford the right kind of top for it. So my dad offered to pay me money if he could throw junk into it because he didn't want to rent a trailer to go to the dump. We buried a bunch of junk in my hole."

"Sure enough does look like a grave to me," she said with resolve. "But it's none of my business, don't you know." She walked back to her house shaking her head. I think for as long as thoughts passed through her mind, she thought there was a strong possibility that someone was buried next door under a six-by-six mound of earth. But it was really just junk.

The thought of the police department digging up a ton of old junk tickled me. I actually hoped that she would call them and they would come out. But of course they never did.

I'm not sure when but I stopped worrying about the bomb and wars, and I never dug a bomb shelter again. I'm not sure why I stopped worrying. Maybe the problem got too big to do anything about. Maybe way down deep I didn't want to be the only one left in an empty town. Maybe I didn't want to be different. Maybe it was all of the above.

Even now I still worry a little bit about dying, because I like living so much, that's why. But unlike then, I'm prepared to die. I have only two worries. One, will it hurt? And two, how will my family do without me? I used to wonder what comes next, but now I know. I found out four years after I filled up the hole in my backyard. That story is up ahead.

8

The Back of the Bus

AFTER FILLING THE BOMB SHELTER, I started to concentrate on living again. It wasn't the length of my life that made any real difference, but the quality of my life. When I looked around I saw everyone making choices as to how they would live their lives. Some of their choices didn't look so good. I couldn't understand how they could live with their choices and feel good at night when they went to sleep.

How people treat other people is very important to me. One of the greatest lessons of my life came in the back of a school bus. It involved a pioneer and the way she was treated by those I called my friends.

Lisbia didn't *look* like a pioneer. She was a reluctant one to be sure. I couldn't help staring at her. Lisbia was a celebrity: the first black girl to go to Elliot Junior High School in Altadena, California. I had never been that close to a black girl my age, and I thought she was pretty.

Lisbia had sparkling dark brown almond-shaped eyes, full of apprehension. She mostly stared at the ground for fear of what she might see in our eyes. When she did look up, our eyes met for just a second, and I smiled so she would know that not everybody at our school hated her just for being black. She looked down again so quickly that I was not sure she had seen me smile. Her white cotton dress had a dainty collar with lots of eyelets and was embroidered with brightly colored flowers. Lisbia was a delicate and very feminine thirteen-year-old girl—a lamb among the wolves as it turned out.

I was fascinated by her hair, wondering if it was as springy as it looked. I thought maybe if we became friends I would ask her if I could press on it to see how it felt. Even I knew that going up to the first black girl that ever went to Elliot Junior High School and saying, "Could I touch your hair?" wasn't cool. So we just waited for the bus while everyone stole glances of Lisbia. We were all in a bunch, except that she stood about ten feet away like that's where she was used to standing. No one thought she was being unfriendly. They knew she was afraid, but nobody made the first move to change things.

THE RELUCTANT PIONEER

The school bus was a few minutes late. Normally the conversation was loud and unrestrained. You remember the way all junior high kids talk when adults aren't around. But that day most of them weren't saying anything. They just stared straight ahead and thought about the implications of this historic day.

They were thinking their parents' thoughts—probably that this shy, frightened, delicate, unassuming, thirteen-year-old black girl and her family were single-handedly responsible for the lowering of property values in the quiet suburban middle to upper middle class community of Altadena. Fortunes were being lost all around us because of her family. Old people were losing their nest egg, their grub stake because Lisbia's family moved in across the street from somebody.

Ground zero must be real close by, within two blocks, otherwise she wouldn't be getting on at our bus stop. We had heard rumors it had finally happened, and Lisbia offered living proof. But as I looked at her, I couldn't bring myself to believe she was bad or had nasty plans for our little community.

We were thinking our parents' thoughts. And why not? If you can't trust your parents, who can you trust? Because of our parents, we knew some things about Lisbia even though we hadn't yet said a word to her. We knew that she could dance real good and that she would light up in the presence of watermelon or fried chicken. We knew she wasn't quite as bright as we were because we all watched "Amos and Andy" on TV. We knew that black people had a distinct odor that was unlike white folks' and more offensive. We knew that black people were basically lazy. We knew that however nice Lisbia's house looked when she bought it, it would soon fall into disrepair and be a blight on the neighborhood. We knew those things because trusted adults had told us. Why wouldn't we believe them?

We would have guessed that Lisbia's father was a doorman at a nice hotel or a cab driver or maybe a custodian, but we would have been wrong. We found out later that he was a rocket scientist who worked at Cal Tech, one of the most respected institutions of higher learning in the world. He was also a consultant to Jet Propulsion Laboratories where the rocket engines were built and tested. Reknowned and respected in his field, Lisbia's dad was born into a rich and successful Panamanian family and educated in the United States. He hung out with the Paulings and the Pickerings and many others who stand tall in the history of space science. We didn't know any of that, so we just imagined that he was a custodian or a garbage man or something no white person would really want to be.

When the bus came, dozens of faces were pressed against the windows on the right side, anxious to see if the rumors were true. They wanted to see if Elliot really was going to get its first black student. I was a little embarrassed for Lisbia when I saw the way that the kids were gawking at her. I was a little embarrassed to be white with my kind acting like that.

Ours was the last pickup point on the route and by that time most of the seats were full. It didn't seem fair, but a good share of the time about half of the people at our stop had to stand up and hold an overhead rail for the four-mile ride to school. When the bus stopped, everyone scurried up the steps. I waited for Lisbia who stared at the ground as she approached the bus. Our eyes met for a moment, and I smiled. She dared a quick smile back and began to ascend the stairs into the bus.

The redneck bus driver turned away in disgust as Lisbia walked toward the back of the bus. There was just one seat left, and Tommy Rand, my bus buddy, was saving it for me. Tommy put his hand on the seat and said in a gruff manner, "It's saved for him," and pointed at me. Had I sat down, Lisbia would have been the only one standing. I just couldn't bring myself to let that happen. Things seemed hard enough for her already. I gestured to the open seat and said, "Please, sit down."

Tommy Rand glared at me, then he glared at her and slid as close to the bus window as he could. Lisbia saw the glare and declined my offer to sit down, but I insisted. She sat down half on and half off the seat, not wanting Tommy to be any more inconvenienced than she perceived him to be. The corners of her eyes were teary, and she just looked ahead for most of the trip. I did chat with her briefly when her tears dried and was entertained by her lilting Panamanian accent. I was more convinced than ever that our community was not going to be injured by Lisbia's arrival. She was a nice girl, no doubt about it.

The bus came to a somewhat jarring stop at school and the kids scrambled off to tell their friends what it was like to ride with a black person. The voice of our school principal, Mr. Dorland, could be heard over the clammer and shouting. He called out, "Slow it down, kids. You're not going to a fire, you know."

He seemed amused with himself for exercising his authority, but everybody else thought, "Boy, what a Bozo!" Mr. Dorland stopped Lisbia when she came down the steps just ahead of me, and I heard him say, "Come with me, dear." I bet he was going to warn her about how hard it was to be the first black person ever to come to Elliot Junior High School in Altadena. Whatever he might have said would have been an underestimation.

I waited at the bottom of the bus steps because Tommy and I always walked to class together. When Tommy got off he slugged me in the arm really hard like he meant business and pushed me aside to tell me off. "You did that on purpose, diphead. Every jerk brain at school is going to call me a nigger lover because of you. I won't forget this, you can count on it." He stormed off to class leaving me a little angry. I was just trying to be nice to Lisbia. It had never occurred to me that Tommy or any of my friends would have felt that way.

SOUTHERN ROOTS

My earliest recollections of my own childhood in the early 1950's should have served as previews of coming attractions. My grandparents and great-grandparents on my mother's side were mostly from the south. And though they were law-abiding, decent people, solid Americans to be sure, they were prejudiced. I never heard them call blacks "niggers," always "negras" or "negroes."

The negroes were a weekly topic of conversation that always revolved around the same theme. My great-grandfather would say, "Heard that a negra family moved in a nice house on 16th street. Why don't they just stick to their own? When we settled here in the thirties we never dreamed they would be getting this close."

My step-grandfather would say, "Six miles from here, Pop, but that don't bother Hazel and me because were moving to Twenty-nine Palms when we retire. Then we'll be 'bout a hundred and fifty miles from 16th street. Why don't you come with us?"

"No, sir," Pop would say, his jaw set firmly. "They ain't gonna run us off that easy. Maybe the folks out here will be kinder to their neighbors and won't sell to the negras." Then Pop would shake his head and ask with grave concern, "Why would any folks want to go live where they weren't really wanted? Don't make no kind of sense to do that. How could someone sell out knowing their friends and neighbors were going to lose a pile of money because of what they did? That don't make no kind of sense. I heard that the negras will pay up to twice as much for a house than it's worth knowing that they can buy the rest of the houses near it for half as much as they're worth. Maybe I'll get lucky an' die before they get to 30th street."

Pop was to get his wish. As he was uttering those words, cancer was spreading throughout his body much faster than the blacks were spreading. Doesn't it seem ironic that he had spent most of the years of his life fearing an event that he never lived to see and was eaten alive by something he never saw?

At any rate, my great grandmother would soon tire of hearing about the black plague—as my family thought of it—

and begin to reminisce about grander times in the south. She was from a somewhat lackluster part of a glorious aristocratic southern family. She loved to talk about it as if she were in the middle of all the glamor, though she was really more off to the side, so to speak.

She would expound, "Now my grandfather was a fine southern gentleman. He was a wealthy landowner in Virginia. Wade Hampton was a Civil War General and a United States Senator. He owned lots a freed slaves, which I used to talk to when I was a little girl. Even after the Civil War was over they stayed with him because he'd been so good to them. They loved him and talked with great respect when they spoke his name out loud."

Then she would go to the closet and bring out his Civil War sword, and I would catch my breath. I believed a hero's sword had a power of its own. My grandmother loved it. Her eyes danced as she remembered her grandfather. I bragged about my great-great-grandfather all of my young life. Anytime any teacher would bring up the Civil War I couldn't shoot my hand up fast enough to tell about my wonderful, famous, great-great-grandfather General Wade Hampton. Then I would tell all about how his slaves loved him and how they stayed to work for him after the war. I was so proud of him.

Then the day came when I went to college and took History 1A. We studied colonial development, the War of 1812, the Gold Rush, and the railroad. I was trembling with excitement as the day finally came when Professor Wilbur Scoggins, maybe the finest teacher I have ever known, began to paint a picture of what he called the darkest period of American history. He was referring to the time when Americans, especially in the south, built their economy on the horrible foundation of slave labor.

I could feel the muscles in my right shoulder tensing up as

I was getting ready to thrust my outstretched hand into the air to enthusiastically signify that I had something important to say. Just before my hand shot skyward I heard some of the most enlightening and deflating words I was ever to hear.

Professor Scoggins began soberly, then angrily, exposing the degradations experienced by blacks as they were kidnapped from their homes in Africa, packed in slave ships like sardines in a can, and brought to America where, for the most part, they were forced to work at breakneck pace from sunup to sundown. They were bred like cattle, and their family units were not considered sacred as we did our own. Parents often watched their children taken to market where they were sold like livestock. Children saw their parents sold down the river never to see them again in this life.

Professor Scoggins' gift of teaching was something to behold. As he spoke we were transported into history. We could smell the degradation, we could feel the anguish, we could taste the hopelessness, and it was bitter on our tongue. Only a handful of teachers could do that, but Professor Scoggins taught with such power and style that he took you along with him and dropped you off just where he thought you should be. He was really something.

Well, I was about ready to share my great-grandmother's sweet, remembrances of her grandfather when Professor Scoggins sighed deeply as though he was overtaken with grief. He began to speak more seriously than before.

Class history can be a drag, let's face it. But history is people and their stories. I think I can best communicate the cruelty and the exploitation involved with the institution of slavery by telling you the story of the man who I believe epitomized the avarice and greed that gave birth to the American aberration of slavery.

This man, in my estimation, was the worst of them all

and has been the subject of a lot of my attention. His name was Wade Hampton. He was a rich and influential man who rose quickly through the south's social and political ranks to become a southern general and even a United States senator. He was the dark symbol of an even darker system. He beat his slaves, bred the females like cattle to black men who were strong and healthy, called bucks. He gave them no right to family and he would shoot them if they dared to run away.

During reconstruction he convinced them that there was nowhere to go, so they had better stick with him, and out of fear of a world that didn't seem to care they stayed. The now Senator Hampton treated them as he always had. It is hard to believe that Wade Hampton was a human being. He certainly wasn't a human in the same context as other men. He falls into the category of inhumane or sub-human.

Professor Scoggins looked as though he wanted to spit out the taste of the very name of Wade Hampton. I couldn't blame him. Needless to say, I have not since raised my hand to laud my heritage. Sometimes the truth hurts. I know it did that day. But I didn't know any of this when Lisbia stood at a lonely bus stop for the first time and I tried to smile at her. I am encouraged that I may be some evidence that changes can take place for the better.

A CUT FLOWER

Lisbia didn't fare well. She lasted just six weeks at Elliot Junior High School—forty-two days for us and about a thousand years for her. I saw every day how sadly alone she was. Some girls invited her to eat lunch with them, but I never saw her with a real friend. Lisbia wilted in six weeks. She was like a cut flower. It was clear to see that she had once bloomed, but in the face of hate and rejection she wilted.

You could see the pain in her eyes and in the way she walked. The last time I looked into her eyes she wasn't home. She was gone to wherever you go to survive when the pain is too much to endure. Her load was just too heavy for her. We heard that her family's life had been threatened several times. One day she just stopped coming to the bus stop. In fact I never saw her again, and nobody ever knew just what happened to her or to her family.

There was a lot of talk. "Well, it's all worked out for the best," kind of talk, but it didn't work out for the best. We weren't better for chasing her off, and she wasn't better for the hurt and rejection she faced. We had all suffered a setback and I'm ashamed that I didn't do more to help her. But I was in the eighth grade and didn't know what to do. I could barely find my way home when I was thirteen. Thirty-four years have marched by or over me. Lisbia's frightened almond eyes still haunt me and prevent me from taking any special pride in being white.

The Bible says that the sins of the parents visit the children until the third and fourth generation. That is right on. From Wade Hampton till this day, prejudice has been losing its filthy grip on my family. I can't say that the urge to feel superior to one ethnic group or another doesn't still crop up. But at least when it does, I can see it for what it is: a filthy lie. Then I can fight the urge off.

I'm committed to keep fighting prejudice whenever I see it eating away at me or seeking to poison others. It's too late to help Lisbia but not too late to help her children or even her grandchildren. I can't change my past, but the future is up for grabs.

0

The Devil's Playground

I DON'T KNOW ABOUT YOU, but left with too much idle time, I am likely to become a public nuisance. It has always been that way for me. One of my father's favorite pithy sayings was, "An idle mind is the devil's playground." Applied to me, it would be better stated, "Gary's idle mind is the devil's national park."

In the seventh grade, I was given the opportunity to join the school orchestra. I really wasn't the orchestra type, but the alternative class had *homework*—to which I was allergic. I followed Mr. Palmer, the aging orchestra director, to the band room where new recruits tried out the different instruments. The violin seemed too feminine. The cello held no appeal, because I knew the boy who would sit next to me, and I had no desire to catch cooties. Then the closet door opened to reveal a string bass. It was love at first sight. When first I plucked the massive strings, I could feel the resonance rumble through my body. This was a man's instrument. I would be a bassist.

In no time Mr. Palmer had an eager crop of seventh graders pulling bows across strings and blowing enthusiastically into wood, chrome, and brass. The ensuing sound was not unlike that produced by a group of children jumping up and down on cats and parrots. When I was young I thought of Mr. Palmer as a dedicated teacher and lover of fine music. As I look back now, I wonder what dark sin he was attempting to atone for by locking himself in a room five hours a day with junior-high musicians.

Orchestra was not always fun and games—not by a long shot. With twenty-one new students, Mr. Palmer's time was very limited. We usually did more waiting than playing while he showed each student what to do with his or her instrument. We were instructed to stand or sit quietly while he worked with the others. For some unknown reason, I had an all-consuming desire to fill silent moments with sound. Sometimes I talked, sometimes I plucked, and occasionally I belched.

Mr. Palmer was a patient man, but he had a line, and when you crossed it—as I did on several occasions—he had a fiendishly effective punishment. I have since wondered why our own prison system has not employed his methods in order to rehabilitate the more hardened criminal.

Whenever I crossed the line, I would be sent to Mr. Palmer's office. I can speak from firsthand knowledge that there is no greater state of boredom that a human being can experience than when left alone for thirty minutes or more in a band director's office. You could go through years of band magazines—all printed in black and white—and never be sure you were not looking at the same one over and over again. I knew in my heart that a picture of Elvis or Fats Domino would never brighten this desolate closet of mediocrity. One day, having again been banished to boredom, I found myself looking around to see if anything new had fallen or been left behind. Perhaps some kindred spirit had hidden a note or something in an attempt to make contact with a fellow inmate. I glanced under Mr. Palmer's desk; all I found there were his marching shoes—old and cracked by the moisture absorbed from years of marching over the dew-covered school football field. The toes were curled up and most of the shoe dye had faded.

My eyes then focused on the wall-mounted pencil sharp-ener, full to the brim with pencil shavings. Something to do, I thought. I will be helpful. I removed the pencil's shaving chamber and reached under the desk to dump the contents into the wastebasket. As I did I was again captured by the rus-tic marching shoes. I looked at the shoes... then the shav-ings... then the shoes. I had found a better place to dump the shavings.

I poured half the contents into each shoe, then carefully lifted each shoe into my lap and packed the shavings firmly into the toe area until I had clearly reduced the size by at least an inch. I replaced the shoes to their place under the desk and giggled, theorizing that this had probably been the coolest event that had ever occurred in this office. I only wished I could be there when Mr. Palmer discovered his shoes were far too tight, but my healthy imagination enabled me to enjoy the thought of it almost as much as the actual experience. The more I thought about it, the funnier it be-came. I actually laughed out loud several times during the rest of the day.

About a week later I discovered just how my joke had gone. As I was leaving band that day, Mr. Palmer grasped my shoulder rather firmly and asked if he might talk to me for just a second. I knew in an instant what we would most likely be talking about.

"Gary, Gary, Gary," he began. "You're not in trouble, but I really must know if my suspicions are correct. Last Friday when I practiced with the band, I put on my marching shoes. They are like old friends to me, you see, and fit perfectly—at least they had until last Friday. That day the toes seemed awfully full." He squeezed my shoulder harder, and just for a second I had the illusion that he was going for my neck.

He continued, "When I removed my shoes my heart sank. You see my wife had given me a special pair of socks made of white Angora wool for my birthday. I have a touch of arthritis and varicose veins, and these socks provided a feeling of warmth and support that makes marching less painful. Those socks are now white with dark gray toes. The dark gray won't wash out, bleach out, or come out with any cleaning fluid known to man. Gary, those socks cost my wife seven dollars (this was in 1956), and she's got fire in her eyes. I'm not going to tell anybody if I find out who put the shavings in my shoe, but Gary, were you the one?"

He looked so hurt as he stared deep into my eyes. Even though I wasn't always good, I wasn't a liar at heart either. I hung my head and said, "Yes, Mr. Palmer, I did it. I'm very sorry. I didn't know I would do so much damage. May I please get you a new pair of socks?"

"No, Gary, I couldn't let you do that. But whatever you do, don't let my wife know that it was you, not if you want to make it to the eighth grade." Mr. Palmer gave my shoulder a final squeeze, a sort of "you're forgiven" squeeze, then walked into his office and sat down slowly at his desk. I sometimes wonder if that was one of the many days he asked himself if teaching was worth it.

I felt terrible. Here was a man who had been nice to me in every way, and during a thoughtless moment, an idle moment, I used my time to hurt him and his wife. I had done this to this wonderful man who put up with me when others had lost the desire.

I wish the story ended there, but ironically it did not. You see, I tried to make amends, but failed to do so. With the best of intentions I decided that I needed to make up for the angora socks I had violated. After a bit of thinking, I decided that I would make him something. An ashtray would have been good, but he didn't smoke. I wanted to give Mr. Palmer something he could be proud of and use daily, so I decided to make him a baton with which he could lead the orchestra.

I made the baton under the supervision of Mr. Domenico,

the wood shop teacher, but I had failed to research baton-making. I used a dowel made of a soft pine, instead of using one made of considerably harder wood like teak or oak or ash. Even though it looked pretty professional, the baton was more fragile than a baton ought to be. The result was humiliating, both to Mr. Palmer and to me. Let me tell you about it.

I presented my gift with these carefully rehearsed words: "Mr. Palmer, I'm really sorry about the socks. And since you wouldn't let me replace them, I thought that I would make something for you in wood shop. I made this baton for you. I hope you like it."

Mr. Palmer was visibly moved. He put his arm around me and gave me a hug. "Thank you, son. Thank you very, very much. I'm moved, genuinely moved. I want you to forget about the socks. As long as I'm wearing shoes, they serve me well. No one would ever know."

As he proudly gazed at the baton, a wheelbarrow full of guilt fell from my shoulders. I walked tall to the closet where my string bass was kept and took my place in the orchestra. I was basking in the radiance of his approval and felt good about the way I had atoned for my sin. It was a short lived feeling, but it got better before it got worse.

Mr. Palmer stood before the orchestra and called out, "Attention ladies and gentlemen, all eyes forward, please. I want to let you know that today I will be leading the orchestra with this beautiful baton Mr. Richmond made for me in wood shop class." I flushed with pride as he held it up for all to see. It looked pretty good.

He continued, "Get out your folders and pull out the little Bach number we have been working on." Then Mr. Palmer tapped three times on his music stand, which was always our sign to assume a playing position and be ready to start on the same note.

On the third tap, the baton broke in two.

There flashed across his countenance a number of expressions, each of which eloquently displayed a road map of his thoughts: dismay, shock, guilt, contemplation, anger, realization, and then resignation. We never talked about it, but I know as sure as I know anything on this earth what was going through his mind. "Oh no, how could this have happened? I just broke Gary's gift in front of forty of his peers. What kind of heavy-handed man would do this to a student? Hey, wait a minute… this was a set-up! Gary is a practical joker. He knew it would break easily. He's seen me break batons before. I should have known."

Mr. Palmer didn't say anything. He just went to his cabinet and pulled out his professionally made baton and tapped three times again with a good deal of force to see if he had treated my baton too roughly. That one held together. Calm settled over his face as we began to mutilate Bach's little classic.

Mr. Palmer was accustomed to our level of ability and seemed to be content with the facsimile of music. He was a wonderful teacher who never gave up on me. In fact, I think I was actually one of his favorites. I loved the string bass and began to play in a little jazz band. "The Informals" played Dixieland Jazz, pop music, and dance tunes. We were the hit of the all-school talent show playing "When the Saints Go Marching In."

I was just one of five orchestra students who did something more than get an easy grade. I really used what he taught me, and Mr. Palmer took a fatherly pride and interest in it. My father even bought me a string bass which I still own.

I know Mr. Palmer always thought the baton thing was a joke. For a long time, I wanted to try to tell him it wasn't but I never did. Too much history would rise up to validate his theory. He died thinking I was a likable rascal.

I had tried to make things right and I had failed. But from that time on, at least in his class, I was a very good student, which is all he really wanted from me. The best repentance is a change of behavior.

10

Rose Ann Lampasona

G ROWING UP IS SUCH A SUBTLE THING, full of surprise and wonder. Much more than the passing of time or a matter of pounds and inches, it is knowledge, perspective, dawning wisdom, and changing feelings. In some ways the process never ends, but certain bench marks and water lines assured me that, like it or not, I was growing up.

One rarely wants to remain a child. I didn't, and now I find that sad. Childhood was a treasure to be spent while it was happening and I failed to value it until it was a sweet memory. Like so many things, I didn't know what I had until it was gone. Once it is gone you own a regret and learn that whatever you are now is God's gift to be opened and cherished in the present—or else your life will be filled with empty yesterdays.

I spent far too much time taking for granted what I had and wanting what would be mine just up the road a ways. I was counted among the boys that wanted to grow up before my time. I felt my world was too full of "you're-too-youngs," forbidden fruit, and stop signs. I saw age as a passkey to unlock the restrictions and encumbrances of youth.

But I didn't miss everything. I remember one of the passages from childhood to adolescence with special fondness. Rose Ann Lampasona helped me realize that I was putting away childish things and becoming a man. She did it without lifting a finger or even being aware that she was doing it.

I met Rose Ann for the first time in Mrs. Warmen's second grade class. We continued to be in classes together all the way through high school. On our first meeting I was taken with her warm smile and willingness to be a friend with the new guy just in from the country. Rose Ann had an infectious laugh, and her voice was deep and always a little hoarse. Strongly built, like a boy should be, she was good at playground sports like softball, kickball, and soccer. What stood out about Rose Ann was her thick head of curly black Italian hair that was already waist length in the second grade. She was one of my best friends, someone who was loyal and cared if I was happy or sad. We enjoyed going over to each other's homes to play. Rose Ann was a tomboy who didn't want to kiss or anything. She just wanted to run, wrestle, push, shove, and laugh lazy afternoons away by the dozens.

As we grew up we sometimes saw older boys and girls together near Elliot Junior High. They would be staring into each other's eyes, holding hands, hugging, and kissing. We always laughed and said "yuck" or "spare me" and wondered why a girl and a boy would want to do those things.

To tell you the truth I had tried kissing once in fifth grade and could not see anything in it. I had another good buddy named Marie Mitchell. One time I asked her if she ever wondered how it felt to kiss like the movie stars kissed, and she said she did. I told her that I had wondered the same thing and asked her if she wanted to try a movie star kiss with me. She said okay.

Neither of us wanted our experiment to be public, so we stepped behind the hedges that surrounded the school buildings I remember my heart was beating with excitement. Marie was pretty daring for a girl. She said, "Well, let's get this over with." I put my arms around her and she put her arms around me and we pressed our little fifth grade lips against each other very tightly and succeeded in pinching each other pretty good.

Marie was the first to speak. "Did you like that?" she asked suspiciously.

"No, it kind of hurt," I answered, patting my lip to see if it was swelling.

"Do you think we did it right?" she explored.

"I don't know. Do you want to try it once more?"

We resumed our movie star postures and kissed once again. This time one of us got spit on the other. That did it, because everybody knows that spit has germs in it, and germs make you sick. We both agreed that kissing was a yucko thing to do. It was quite some time before I tried it again and struck gold. But at age ten something is not yet connected. Try as you may, kissing is not fun.

I never tried to kiss Rose Ann. The thought never occurred to me while we were growing up. Then came the summer that followed our seventh grade year when I didn't see her for three months. Rose Ann changed, great changes which had a strange effect on me whenever I looked at her, which I did a lot. She seemed to appreciate them as well because she wore clothes that emphasized her new curves.

Rose Ann wore makeup and earrings and was shaped entirely differently than she had been just three months before. She had places where no places had been before. It was a miracle! Rose Ann suddenly looked like a young woman and made me feel different than I had ever felt. Gone was the desire to play kickball or soccer or play hide-and-go-seek. I would now gladly just sit next to her and maybe hold hands, and then talk about how pretty she had become.

Up to this point in my life, I could not imagine anything more exciting than catching a snake or a lizard or a shark. Now I could.

I wondered how I looked to Rose Ann. My voice was changing and I was wearing my hair in a Balboa, flat on top and long on the sides. The hair on the sides was combed up to look like a wave breaking and came together in what was called a jelly roll in the middle of my forehead. It was an "in" hair cut in the fifties, and I wondered if she thought I was cool. She still seemed to be a good friend, but I was pretty sure that she was not experiencing the same chemistry that I was experiencing. I was hoping that she didn't notice that I could barely keep myself from staring at her all the time.

I was glad that I was seated just behind Rose Ann in eighth grade math. I could flirt with her pretty much every day. The first three months of school I just kept saying, "Boy, you sure changed over the summer, Rose Ann." Then she would ask what I meant, and I was in trouble. I knew it would be tacky to say, "Your new shape is great," or "Makeup makes you really pretty." So usually I just said, "Oh, I don't know. You just look great."

She liked it when I said that because it produced one of her patented infectious laughs. Her voice was still hoarse but now I would call it sexy. Anyway I made a profession out of getting her attention because I enjoyed how it made me feel. This habit nearly got me kicked out of school.

One day I reached into the pocket of my jeans and felt the usual supply of rubber bands and paper clips. I suddenly had a great idea. I wove several of the rubber bands together until they were about ten inches long. Then I quietly attached it to the top slat on the back of Rose Ann's desk chair. I pulled on it to see what kind of tension it would develop. It felt just right for what I was trying to do.

I reached back into my pocket and located a paper clip and bent it open to form a hook. I attached the paper clip to the rubber bands and gently slipped the paper clip through the zipper of Rose Ann's dress. My theory was that at the end of class when Rose Ann stood up, the rubber bands would tighten and then pull down the zipper of her dress. It was one of those jokes that you really don't think will work, when you think that imagining will be better than the result. Boy, was I ever wrong! No theory of physics was ever proven more conclusively than my theory of the effect of rubber band tension on a dress zipper.

When I placed the paper clip in the zipper, we still had about fifteen minutes of class left. We were doing math exercises when my pencil broke. I slipped out of my chair and went to the pencil sharpener. I ground the tip of my number two yellow pencil to a lethal sharpness, which I tested with my finger. Satisfied, I returned to my desk.

Just as I slipped into my chair Rose Ann stood up. You could hear the whirrrrr of her zipper opening throughout the quiet room. Everyone turned to look. Every eye was instantly on Rose Ann as she became aware that the back of her dress was now wide open. The silky white slip she had donned that morning was now on display for the world to see.

There was nothing cheap or sleazy about Rose Ann Lampasona, and the degree of her modesty was demonstrated by the intensity of her scream. I felt panicked. For a brief moment I thought about trying to pull the zipper back up. I even began to reach for it and decided such action might inspire even more modesty, and I had inspired enough.

Our teacher leapt to his feet, for it sounded more serious and life-threatening than it was. Mr. Raleigh was a stern man, a person without humor who didn't like junior high students. He was boring and hard to listen to for forty-five minutes a day. He seemed resigned to his fate yet bitter, anxious to unleash his anger and wreak vengeance on any youth that failed to convince him that he was living a meaningful life. I wondered why Mr. Raleigh hadn't left teaching years before.

I did reach out and snap the rubber band apart. The now hysterical Rose Ann Lampasona ran into the cloak closet to zip up her dress. She was joined by two girlfriends who comforted her.

Mr. Raleigh came slowly to the scene of the crime and held my eyes with his menacing, unflinching stare. He wore the thickest glasses that I have ever seen in my life. They made you dizzy to look into and reduced the size of his pupils. His eyes looked beady and expressionless, even reptilian and predatory. Mr. Raleigh looked down at the rubber bands on the back of Rose Ann's chair. Then he lifted the rest of them from my hands and stared at the paper clip attached to them and reasoned what I had done.

He pursed his lips together, his eyes narrowed to malevolent slits. Then Mr. Raleigh said with venom and vengeance, "Mr. Richmond, I hope you have derived satisfaction from your humiliation of Miss Lampasona. It's time that you receive what's due you. I wish for you to get up immediately and report to Mr. Noreen, the vice principal. You explain to him what you have done. Then I will be talking to him to see if you have reported your degradation with sufficient gravity. Go now!"

I stood up, my mind already racing to the most important of all thoughts: "My dad's going to kill me." I walked slowly to the vice principal's office. No need to walk fast. When I got there all three of the secretaries looked up and smiled. Mrs. Prentice asked with genuine enthusiasm, "Gary, what did you do this time?" The other ladies laughed and stopped what they were doing. I had been pretty entertaining before and they didn't want to miss a chance for a good story.

I shared in detail what I had done. Before I was finished, two of the secretaries were laid out on their desks out of breath from laughing. Mrs. Prentice was Mr. Noreen's secretary, so she felt an obligation for more decorum, but she could not help herself from fighting back a smile. She slid back her chair and stood up. "Mr. Noreen will see you in a moment. Why don't you sit down for a moment, Gary."

She walked to his office and leaned in. She didn't know it but I heard her laugh and say, "Mr Richmond is here to see you, Mr. Noreen. You're going to love this one! It's the best yet." The conversation got quieter and I couldn't understand what was being said, but it was punctuated with occasional laughter. I began to have hope that I might not get kicked out of school.

Mr. Noreen came out of his office smiling. He just sat down next to me and asked me to tell him why Mr. Raleigh had sent me to the office. He smiled through the whole explanation even though I didn't try to make it funny. In fact I told him it was important to Mr. Raleigh that I report the story of my degradation with sufficient gravity.

He laughed and said, "What?"

"I think he wants me to see how bad I was so I won't do it again, which I won't, Mr. Noreen. Really!"

"I can see you are truly sorry, Gary. Sounds to me like one of those jokes that just gets out of control. Went farther than you wanted it, right son?"

"Yes sir, that's exactly what happened. Rose Ann's my friend since second grade, and I wouldn't hurt her feelings for anything. I'm going to apologize to her as soon as I can."

"Gary, to tell you the truth I don't have it in my heart to punish you. I don't think Mr. Raleigh is famous for his sense of humor. Although I wouldn't want to see you in here again for such a prank, I think all you meant to do was to play a joke. Why don't you come in here the next two days? I'll tell Mr. Raleigh that you explained your degradation with sufficient gravity. Does that sound fair to you?"

"Yes, sir. Does this mean that my dad doesn't have to know I got in trouble in math class?"

"I don't see any reason to tell your father about this, Gary."

"Thank you, Mr. Noreen. You've been very nice to me." Mr. Noreen didn't make me miss all my classes for two days, just Mr. Raleigh's. It was a favor really. I hated math, and it gave Rose Ann time to forgive me, which she freely did. We were friends and always will be in my memory. She was more than friends. She was a gift that introduced me to new stirrings that would increase my ability to love and bond.

Rose Ann Lampasona was the first woman to make me feel like a man. You know what I mean? Sigh! Some people hate this part of growing up. I loved it.

11

The Shot Put

JUNIOR HIGH SCHOOL introduced me to a new kind of class called electives, classes that you didn't have to take unless you wanted to. Ninety-nine percent of the time, girls would choose to take homemaking, chorus, and typing. At that time it was well accepted that girls would like to be housewives, secretaries, or lounge singers. Of course there was the occasional boy who would sign up for these courses as a joke, or because he couldn't face a whole period of the school day separated from his girlfriend—who he usually broke up with before the third week of class.

Real men took shop. There was wood shop, metal shop, and photography. Shop teachers didn't pretend to be academics. Ours was the consummate shop teacher. He had missing teeth, a beer belly that created speculation concerning pregnancy, a shiny bald head, hairy arms, and an indomitable smile. He usually had six junior high boys hanging all over him hoping he would swear or tell a dirty joke. Mr. Domenico was his name, and he loved kids because even at forty-five, he was still a kid at heart.

Mr. Domenico gave us all names like Bozo, Jerko, Stupid, and Blockhead. Nobody was ever insulted. In fact if he called us by our real names we wondered if maybe we had done something wrong. At the end of the semester he just gave everyone an A or a B. His B's would have been F's in anyone else's class. Only total losers who never obeyed the safety rules ever got on his bad side. But Mr. Domenico was forgiving. You had to work hard at staying on his bad side because he worked hard to keep you off it.

You know how much he loved kids? He volunteered for lunch duty so he could be with us some more. And he was so popular even the girls would come and talk to him, which made us a little jealous because he was our teacher.

The girls had Mrs. Thompson for homemaking. She also liked kids and was pleasant. She talked in a singsong voice, assumed feminine postures a lot, and wore her hair in a bun. She was proper and elegant in her own way, consumed with the challenge of helping seventh grade girls become ladies. When you got out of her class you knew which fork to use at a gala affair and how to make clothing that would cover everything but your face.

I always imagined that if you married a homemaking teacher you'd eat well. Mrs. Thompson was certainly eating well but she wore dresses that were slimming. Besides, she was so nice that no one ever really cared how many chocolate chip cookies she was sampling during and after class. Her class sure smelled better than shop class, that's for sure.

Well, back to the story about how I found a way to link gym class to shop class—metal shop to be exact. You see, I was a shot-putter. That means that I would stand at the back of a ring about five feet across and tuck a ten-pound iron ball under my chin. Then I would lurch forward, build momentum, and push that iron ball with all of my strength and weight. If I was lucky it would go more than forty feet and I would place first, second, or third in the track meet. I always wished that I was stronger or that the shot put was lighter.

In metal shop we got into casting aluminum. Mr. Domenico showed us how to make forms out of damp sand. Say you wanted to make an aluminum apple. You would put damp sand in a twelve by twelve by twelve box that was hinged in the middle, just enough sand to set the apple on. You would pack the damp sand as hard as you could in layers until you had covered the apple. Then you would take a very thin knife and run it through a slit in the box until you could open the mold and remove the apple.

Then you closed the mold and inserted a tube into which you would poor molten aluminum. After filling the mold, you would give it plenty of time to cool and harden. Then you could reopen the mold and take out your aluminum reproduction of an apple. It was great, except with a world of things you could make, most junior high boys made their parents ash trays—whether or not their parents smoked.

One day when I was practicing the shot put, I suddenly looked at it and realized that it must have come into existence by the very same process that we had learned in metal shop. It had been cast. I thought to myself, "Self, wouldn't it be funny to make an aluminum shot put? It would weigh about one third the weight of the real thing, and you could put it a mile. You'd look like Super Boy."

"Mr. Domenico," I asked, holding a real shot put in front of his face. "Could we cast an aluminum shot put?"

He rolled it around in his hands, looking at it from all angles. "No problem," he said with a smile. "But before we do, I'd like to know just how you're planning on using it. If it involves cheating, count me out."

"Oh no, sir, nothing like that."

"You just want to impress the coach, maybe get an A in track and field?"

"Mr. Domenico, I was just planning on playing a joke on the coach. I wouldn't cheat or nothin' like that."

"Well, Blockhead," he said with a twinkle in his eye. "Count me in. Is it Coach Matuzak you're going to nail?"

"Yes, sir."

"You'll give me all the details?"

"You bet."

Mr. Domenico threw his head back and laughed a belly laugh as he imagined the coach's amazement when I broke an Olympic record. He didn't even think of letting me do the casting. He wanted it to be his work of art. And it was. When Mr. Domenico got done it looked so real no one could tell the aluminum shot put from the real McCoy. He held them next to each other and giggled a little boy's diabolical giggle. "Bozo, I wish I could be there to see the expression on Matuzak's face when you toss this baby farther than he could toss the real thing. But if I were there, Matuzak might figure out what was going on. Son, this was a real good idea. Sure wish I could be there."

I took the aluminum shot put to practice and waited for the coach to come by the shot put ring. When he did I said, "Coach, could you show me proper form again? I think I'm slipping, and it would really help me if I could watch you put it out there. Give it your best shot, coach."

Coach Matuzak was your basic macho gym coach and anxious to look good whenever given the opportunity. He said, "Sure, man. Gary, what's your best put?"

"Forty-four feet and seven inches, coach," I answered humbly. He smiled. I handed him the ten pounder, and he bounced it from hand to hand to stretch his fingers and get ready for his best effort. As he did he explained the theory of using the weight of your whole body to push the shot as far as possible.

Coach Matuzak stepped into the ring still rocking the heavy shot back and forth. Then he got serious. He tucked the shot put under his chin and bent down, putting most of his weight on his right foot. He bobbed up and down as he prepared to let one fly. All of a sudden he scooted forward and exploded with a mighty push—a loud ooooof accenting his Herculean effort.

The shot arched high and fell to the ground with a thud. It left a clear round dent in the ground past the forty-five foot mark. You could tell he was pleased with his effort, measuring forty seven feet and four inches. He smiled and said, "Did you watch me, Gary? Did you pick up anything helpful?"

"You bet, coach. Could you stay and see if I do it right, Mr. Matuzak? You might see what I keep doing wrong."

"That's what I'm here for, man," said coach. He smiled.

As arranged, Dave Morgan handed me the aluminum shot put, and I treated it as though it weighed a ton. I rolled it back and forth as coach had, letting him know I was observing safe technique to avoid straining muscles and tendons in my hands, wrists, and arms. I breathed deep as if I were preparing to break a record.

Then I stepped into the ring and bobbed as though I was psyching up for my effort. The coach nodded his approval. I exploded forward, launching the lighter shot put through the air. It arched high and landed about two feet past his effort. Coach Matuzak stared in disbelief. The smile was gone. He recovered and said, "Great effort, Gary." It measured forty-nine feet and one inch.

I spoke humbly, "Coach, you really helped me. I owe it to you. Sorry I beat you, but you could probably do better. Why don't you try again?"

Dave Morgan handed him the ten pounder and the coach stepped back into the ring. Coach Matuzak looked deadly serious and there was no doubt he meant business. He exploded again, only besting his first effort by three inches. He broke out in a cold sweat, feeling humiliated in front of his boys.

"Come on, coach, try again," goaded Dave Morgan. His next effort did not equal either of his first two distances. He looked exasperated and mumbled, "Gary, with a toss like that you could win the all-city meet. That was really good, man."

I didn't have the heart to leave him in such a depleted state. Besides, I could never come near that toss with a real shot put. I asked, "Could I bother you to watch me just one more time? You helped me so much the first time, maybe you could help me some more."

"Sure, Gary. Give it one more go."

I gave it a real ride the next time and it sailed more than seventy feet. Mr. Matuzak's jaw dropped. Then suspicion spread over his face like a forest fire. "What the... nobody your age could toss like that! What gives?"

All of the guys were in on it. We all laughed our heads off as we handed him the fake shot put and explained how Mr. Domenico had helped us to make an aluminum shot put as long as we promised never to use it to cheat. Coach laughed, his sense of masculinity restored.

"Great joke, guys. This looks just like the real thing. You had me all the way." Coach looked behind us at the concrete steps that led to the gate that opened onto the street adjacent to the school. He smiled again, only twice as big as before.

"You guys are going to get a little more mileage out of your joke than you thought. Next week at about this time, the bus from Washington Junior High School is going to park just outside that gate and their whole team is going to march down those steps. You know what they're going to see? A world class shot putter, that's what! Might just make them a little edgy to see that we have that kind of power in the field events." Coach laughed as he walked off to tell the other two coaches what we had done.

Washington was a mostly black school which usually beat us bad in the track meets. But this year we had a terrific team and were competitive in most events. It might be fun to start the meet off with a good joke.

Friday came and coach stood by us waiting for the Washington team to arrive. Finally we heard the rumble of their bus' diesel engine. Amidst clouds of belching diesel smoke, they parked at the top of the stairs and stood behind their coach who began to march the whole group down.

Coach Matuzak whispered, "Get ready."

He got their attention by yelling, "GO FOR IT!" really loud. The whole team stopped to see what I was going to do. I bent down and launched forth with a mighty explosive effort. I ooofed as loud as I could, and the aluminum shot put arched higher and farther than they had ever thought possible. They all gasped audibly and were then struck silent at the superhuman feat of strength they had just witnessed.

Coach Matuzak turned to their coach and said, smiling, "And would you believe he's my second man?" Their coach whistled and shook his head. He looked back at his team and said, "Come along, guys. It looks like we got work to do."

The Washington shot putters stayed behind with us at the shot put ring. Their best man came up to me and said, "I'd sure be happy to know your secret, man."

I laughed and said, "It's easy. I found the ten pound shots to be a little on the heavy side, so we made one that weighs three. You want to try it?" I tossed it to him like a tennis ball and when he caught it he understood my great accomplishment. He laughed and said, "Good joke, man." Then he ran off to tell his coach they were still in the meet.

I'll never forget the moment we stopped the whole team on the stairs. There was a world of difference between what they saw and what they thought they saw. But what they thought they saw made them feel they could not win. They were beaten in their minds.

Man, I loved the memory of that day. Between Rose Ann Lampasona and the male bonding that was taking place on the track team, I was feeling more and more like a man. More like, but not yet a man. At age thirteen, you're on the road but something tells you you're not there yet.

I did a lot of nutty things in my attempt to become a man. One of my many rights of passage took place in a nearby canyon when I foolishly risked my life for no good reason. That's so easy for me to say now, but then I really thought I was proving something. I've confessed the whole fiasco in the next chapter.

12

Eaton Canyon

MALE PRIDE IS A TERRIBLE THING, displayed as either rigid stubbornness or unnecessary acts of foolhardy bravery. I myself have suffered from a megadose of male pride since childhood, and probably will right up to my last hurrah. I expect my gravestone to read, "Loving Husband, Loving Father, Real Bozo."

Male pride has two components: first, a feeling deep inside that you have something to prove; second, the confidence that you have what it takes to prove it. Mixing these two components inevitably causes major damage. This formula can lead you to some pretty bizarre and even life-threatening moments. If you don't get a handle on male pride, you can plan on keeping an early appointment with the funeral director.

When I was thirteen, male pride got the best of me. Frankly, it's surprising that I reached fourteen. It all began when Ronald Larson suggested that we hike to Henniger Flats, along with my best buddy, Doug Sigler, and his best friend, Joey Jordan. The four-mile hike produced a minimum reward: a view of the San Gabriel Valley, Los Angeles, the Pacific Ocean, and Catalina Island if the smog was light. The whole hike was in chaparral, the closest of the environments to desert. It was not really worth it, but at least you could tell all your friends that you walked uphill for four miles.

We left my house at about nine in the morning and proceeded across Mendocino Street, memory lane for me. We passed Patty Mackin's house, the first girl I ever had a severe crush on. And believe me, it was industrial strength. I puppy-loved her so hard my hair hurt. Her family was well to do and lived just above the country club. My dad referred to that part of town as the other side of the tracks, the good side. Patty was nice to me in the same way that Cinderella was nice to Gus the mouse, but she didn't give me a second thought or the time of day. I always wished I was a handsome prince with a glass slipper when I walked by her house, but I was just me and I sighed and trudged on.

As we walked by the Altadena Town and Country Club, we could hear children taking swimming lessons at the Olympic-size pool. That's where I jumped from a high dive for the first time, on the dare of a friend who had invited me to the club as a guest. It was fun except I got half the water in the pool up my nose so that my sinuses burned for the rest of the day.

We passed the mansion of Leo Carillo, who had played the part of Pancho, the Cisco Kid's sidekick. They were major TV stars in the fifties, the Hispanic version of the Lone Ranger and Tonto. Several doors up we passed Victor Mature's, a major leading man in the fifties. I was good friends with his daughter Helen Carter. We went all through elementary school together and I went over to her house to play a few times, but only met her father once and only long enough to shake his hand. He was gone most of the time.

Then we veered north and in two blocks found ourselves staring down into Eaton Canyon. A fire road met us at the top of the western rim and bade us begin our journey to Henniger flats. A big steel bar prevented cars from entering the trail, but at the time it was open to hikers. We descended about two hundred yards where we came to one of our favorite spots: the bridge that spanned the canyon and connected the fire road to its opposite side. A stream rushed under it and disappeared about a mile southwest in the alluvial fan of dirt, sand, and rock that spread out below the canyon.

We couldn't resist going down to the stream for a drink of water—the last water we'd see until we got to the ranger's station at Henniger Flats. That day was going to be a scorcher, so we went down to tank up. It would be about an hour and a half and a gallon of perspiration until the next water stop.

As we took the trail down to the stream we passed the cable car, stationed there to ensure that no one was stranded in need of medical help in case the bridge washed out in a flood or crumbled in an earthquake. It was always locked to a big brass ring anchored in a block of cement and held fast to the western side of the canyon by a chain. The cable car wasn't motorized but the hand-over-hand kind, with room for just four passengers.

We were in no hurry so we piled into the car, pretending we were in a big disaster. Then something happened that had never happened before. The weight of our bodies caused the cable to sag, and the car began to roll forward.

Ronald yelled, "FAR OUT!" and screamed with joy as we rolled quickly out to the middle of the canyon. The span was about one hundred feet and we stopped rolling about halfway. We all looked down as the breeze cooled our faces and fluttered our hair. Wow! The view took your breath away. Being suspended between the two walls of the canyon about forty-five feet up was really something. I could feel my heart kick it up a notch. Directly below us the shallow stream rippled cheerfully to its date with oblivion. Sand and granite rocks of various sizes were really all that lay below us.

"Let's pull it to the other side," said Ron. He was the leader because he was fifteen and a take-charge sort of a guy. We all pulled until we reached the other side. Ron jumped out and held the car in place. He stared down at the rocks. His eyes sparkled—the way a man's eyes sparkle when he thinks he's got a terrific idea.

"Anybody got a watch?" he asked excitedly. Doug did. "Let's see how long it takes to go across if we just go across normally."

"Why?" I asked suspiciously.

"I want to see something," answered Ron.

I didn't pursue it farther. I knew he would reveal his plan soon enough. We got back in the gondola and Ron said, "Go!" We pulled hand over hand at a steady rate and covered the distance in fifty-eight seconds.

"How do you suppose the gondola got loose?" Doug asked.

Ron got out and examined the chain. "Looks like someone hack-sawed it, then tied it together with a string that broke when we piled in," he answered, holding up the chain, and a piece of string was still tied to it. We could also see the shiny marks of where someone had sawed through.

"We'll leave it like we found it so we can come back," Ron added. "But first I want to try something. I'm going to hang from the bottom of the gondola, and you guys pull me across."

His friend Joey said, "Ron, you've done some dumb stunts since we've been friends, but this would be the dumbest stunt of all."

"Listen, I know I can do it because in gym class we had to hang from a steel bar for five minutes to pass a strength test. I did it easy. I could have hung there five more minutes if I had to. We just pulled this thing across the canyon in less than a minute. It's no big deal. Just don't stop, okay?"

I had done the same test and passed it easy, so I thought it would be a piece of cake. In fact, if Ron did it I planned to do it. Of course if he fell and died I could reconsider.

Ron took off his white tee shirt and used it to wipe the steel bar clean of anything slippery. Then he grabbed a handful of dust and rubbed it into his palms to remove any excess oil. He climbed down to a rock just four feet below the gondola and asked us to move the cable car into place so he could get a grip on the cross bar. It was actually the foot rest, so he warned us that he wouldn't take it lightly if anyone stepped on his fingers.

We slowly pulled the cable car gondola into place and Ron grabbed the bar, adjusted his hands, and set his jaw with a determined, "I'm going to do it" look. "Go for it!" he yelled and held onto the bar so hard that his knuckles turned white.

We pulled steadily, and in seconds he was suspended forty-five feet above the rocky stream bed. That would be more than four stories high. Ron "YAHOOED" all the way to the other side and even looked up with a cocky smile right in the middle, where a fall would probably have killed him. When we got to the other side Ron yelled, "Yeah, man! No pickin' sweat!" Then he climbed up next to us and asked, "Who goes next?"

"I go," I blurted out.

I did all the things Ron had done. I wiped off the bar. I rubbed the oil off my hands with sand and had them move the car slowly into place. I adjusted my grip and yelled, "Go!"

Suddenly I was suspended in space. I had a queasy feeling in my stomach and was immediately sorry I had decided to go with the big boys. I heard Ron whisper, "Let's stop it for just a second and scare him."

Right in the middle they stopped the cable car. I talked to myself. "Don't look down. You got plenty of time. Don't give them the satisfaction of being shook." I looked up into three impish faces smiling demonically down at me and said sarcastically, "Any time now."

The gondola moved forward again and my journey was accomplished with relative ease, but I would never do it again on a bet. The daredevil crossing had left me with an empty feeling, even though I bragged about it plenty later and always exaggerated how long they had stopped. I always made the ten seconds sound more like five minutes because it made the story better. Anyway, ten seconds seems like five minutes when you are in danger of falling to your death.

After Joey took his turn, my friend Doug wisely declined.

He took a ribbing for it but not from me. I admired him for it. Doug often used more common sense than I did, and that was probably one of the reasons I hung out with him. I needed to be around someone with a more highly developed capacity for reason.

Ron decided to end our adventure on a high note and asked us if we would take him for a round trip there and back again. He was one of those guys who was into one-up-manship. We all protested, saying things like you don't have anything to prove and maybe you'll wear out on the last trip. But it didn't phase him; he just said, "Let's do it!"

So we went for it. I bet he still thinks about that final ride in his worst dreams. I know I do.

We launched and Ron hollered joyfully and even added a twist by swinging back and forth. His gyrations made it harder for us to pull but he was having fun. We reached the other side and he turned around to face forward and said, "Let's go home," meaning take him back to the other side.

We pulled steadily until we reached the middle. Then Joey stopped it for a second to play the same joke on Ron that he had played on me. Ron looked up, frowned, and laughed, and just waited for us to go. Joey didn't make him wait too long and started pulling. But he hadn't been watching his fingers; he had been watching Ron. We watched in horror as Joey pulled the gondola right over his fingers and got his hand mangled in the mechanism.

Joey screamed out with pain and was unable to get his fingers free. They were being smashed from the weight of all four of us and the gondola. We couldn't go forward or backward without making him scream.

"What's wrong up there?" yelled Ron from below.

"Joey's got his hand caught in the wheels on the cable."

"Get them out! I can't hang here that much longer."

"We're doing everything we can," I yelled back. Joey was turning pale and looked like he was going to pass out from the pain. I stood up to see how his hand was caught. It looked as though we would have to back the gondola over his fingers to get them free. I yelled at Doug to pull hard but when we did Joey screamed so loud that we backed off.

Ron yelled louder than before to get the car moving or he would be spread all over the rocks below shortly. Nobody was checking the time, but I'm sure we had been stopped in the middle at least two minutes. Ron was hanging with his eyes closed concentrating, his knuckles ashen white.

I looked at Doug. "We don't have any choice, Doug. We got to get that wheel over his fingers. Pull with all your might no matter what happens or Ron will be splattered all over those rocks down there." We both looked down and saw Ron hanging limp. We could see he had reached the point of severe testing. His jaws were squeezed together so tightly it looked like he'd be breaking teeth soon.

Doug and I grabbed the cable and pulled for all we were worth. Joey screamed and we pulled harder. We felt the wheel ride up over his fingers. Joey was in total agony, but the wheel cleared and he pulled his bloody fingers to his chest and slumped to the seat.

Doug and I continued to pull, being careful not to get our fingers stuck. We didn't even look down. We just wanted the gondola to hit the other side soon.

We felt the car lighten and for a second were convinced that Ron had fallen to his death. When we hit the other side a second later, Doug and I looked over the side. Ron was laying in the dirt below, looking up at us with a grateful smile. We looked at Joey. He was in a ton of pain and his fingers looked really ugly and mashed. He had tears in his eyes but was not sobbing. We figured he was hurting pretty bad.

Ron helped his friend out of the cable car and led Joey down to the stream where they soaked his fingers for several minutes. When the blood was cleaned off they didn't look so bad. The doctor later determined that he hadn't even broken any fingers. He did lose two fingernails.

The story his parents got was that his fingers had been smashed in a car door at Ron's house while they were horsing around. We never made it to Henniger Flats, but we had learned a valuable lesson at the cable car. Do something really stupid and you can get yourself killed while proving nothing except that you're really stupid. Lots of kids like Doug just kind of knew that. Guys like Ron and me had to prove it for ourselves.

Rites of manhood seem to be an ancient characteristic, a common thread that binds men together. They are also sadly one of the evidences that though we are not the weaker sex, we are definitely the weaker-minded. The old idea of bravery equaling manhood is one I was not able to shake for years to come.

As I look back, I'm not sure that manhood was the only issue. We were also confronting our mortality. I think we were in our own way seeking relief from the terrible idea that we were going to die someday. If death didn't get us today, then maybe it never would—an easier illusion to create in early adolescence than in your mid-forties. I took a bundle of chances and all of them put together never proved that I was a man or immune from death.

I later found my manhood in a peculiar place and was set free from the fear of death in a most surprising way. I still like to take calculated risks—more back-threatening than life-threatening. Now I do it for fun. It's a wonder that I'm still here.

13

Be Sure Your Sins Will Find You Out

WHEN MY FRIEND MIKE MEAGHER'S PARENTS left for a weekend trip, they were wise to issue this warning, which I heard with my own ears. "Michael," his father began, "I was young once, and once I had a learner's permit, just as you have one now.

"There came a point, when, like you, I felt it was ludicrous to wait one moment longer to get my real driver's license. That was because I felt that my driving skills were adequately developed, nicely honed, and perfected for the streets. And they may have been, but the fact remained that the State of California has made it clear, crystal clear, that you don't drive without a valid California driver's license.

"So even though I was tempted, I waited until I had that valid driver's license in my hand before I drove without an adult. I did not jeopardize my parents' standing in the community, nor did I threaten the final act and privilege of receiving a valid license.

"Mike, don't drive your mother's car while we are gone. You don't want to know what we'll do to you if you do. We love you, son. See you on Sunday night. Emergency numbers are on my desk. And Gary, you have a great weekend too. It's good weather for swimming and with three swimming pools on the cul-de-sac, you guys should be wrinkled as prunes when we get back."

We waved goodbye as Mr. and Mrs. Meagher's Cadillac Brougham convertible rounded the top of the hilly cul-de-sac and turned east to head for Palm Springs. It was a beautiful car, robin's egg blue with a white top, and heads turned to look at it wherever you went. I loved riding in it just to see what it must feel like to be rich.

Mike said, "Let's go in the house for fifteen minutes. It would be just like my dad to run to the market or something and come back to see if I'm driving my mom's car."

"What are we going to do after fifteen minutes?" I asked naively.

"We're going to drive my mom's car!" Mike said emphatically.

"Aren't you afraid of what your dad will do to you?"

"No way. My dad did all sorts of crazy stuff when he was our age. He tells me all about it when he gets drunk. Then he forgets he told me. He *expects* me to do some crazy things because he did."

"My dad was a little crazy too, but he won't let me get away with it. He says to me, 'Gary, it seems to be the scheme of things that it's your job to think of stupid things to do and my job to keep you from doing them. You got a bum deal, son. You want to know why? Because I did all the stupid things. That makes me an expert at catching you and don't you forget it.'"

Mike laughed and said, "You still do a lot of stupid things."

"It's my job," I said with a smile. "But my dad does seem to catch me a lot."

Fifteen minutes passed and Mike's parents didn't return. He rubbed his hands together gleefully. "This is the moment

I've been waiting for! My first joy ride."

We opened the garage door, and there in the dim light sat our ticket to adventure. The shiny 1957 black lacquered Packard convertible beckoned to us to come and drive. "Joy for the taking," it whispered. "Feel my power. Know the joy, the freedom of the open road. Go impress some girls," it continued. I'm talking irresistible, industrial strength temptation. We could hardly breathe we were so excited.

We got in and Mike slipped the key into the ignition. "Shoot!" he exclaimed. "Shoot, shoot, shoot, shoot!" he added.

"What's wrong?" I asked without a clue.

"I'll tell you what's wrong and why my dad didn't come back and check on us. The flipping gas gauge reads below empty! It doesn't look like it will go a block on the fumes left in the tank. He probably laughed his picking head off after he got through with his little car speech."

Mike laid his head on the steering wheel and thought. "I got an idea," he blurted out after sitting bolt upright. He jumped out of the car and I followed him one house up the steep cul-de-sac to Dave Donner's house. We knocked on the door and found that Dave was still in his pajamas. In fact we had awakened him at eleven in the morning.

"Listen, Dave. I need some gas. I'm taking the Packard for a joy ride, and my dad ran the gas below empty before they left for Palm Springs."

Dave was still waking up. He said, "Mike, I don't have any gas. We have a gardener, so we don't even keep a can of gas in the garage."

"Dave, I know that. But I know your tank is full because I was with you when you filled it last night."

"So?" said Dave, still disoriented.

"So, we are going to syphon gas out of your tank into the Packard's tank."

"How are we going to do that?" asked Dave.

"I'll push the Packard out of my garage and park it. Then

you back your Chevy out of your garage and park it. I'll get a garden hose and put it in your tank and suck on it until we get the syphon going and when we get a few gallons we'll pull the syphon."

Dave scratched his head and said, "Won't hurt to try, I guess." He got dressed while Mike and I pushed the Packard out of the garage and set the seventy-five foot garden hose in place. Mike was nervous as he waited for Dave to finally get dressed and pull his car out of the garage.

Mike stood there tapping his foot. "Dave's a nice guy but he's a little slow. He's got two speeds—slow and stop."

I laughed and said, "Mike, it's only been five minutes."

Mike looked exasperated like he hadn't heard me and said, "My folks are going to get to Palm Springs and back before he gets out here."

Dave finally came out without having combed his hair, evidence he had hurried. He backed his metallic green '59 Chevy out of the garage and parked it. Mike could hardly pull the gas cap off fast enough. He shoved the garden hose down the fill hole until he could hear the metal tip tapping around in the tank. Then we ran nearly seventy-five feet down to the Packard where Mike sucked and sucked trying to get the syphon going. He turned red sucking his brains out, but not one drop of gas came out of his end of the hose. I tried with the same results.

Dave came down and scratched his head. "We need to prime the syphon," he said.

"What does that mean?" Mike asked.

"Well, if we fill the hose with water—except for the part we stick in my tank—and then let the water run out, it will suck the gas out of my tank. When the water runs out at this end, then you stick the hose in your tank and we'll let it run for awhile."

I could see the logic in that but I had some questions.

"Dave, when do you know for sure the water is done running out and gas begins? If you put water in a gasoline engine you can wreck it."

Dave looked amazed that I would ask. "Anybody can tell the difference between gas and water. Gas looks golden brown. Water's clear. You can also get down close to it and smell it. When we smell gas we'll pick up the hose and shove it in the Packard's tank."

Dave seemed so confident it never occurred to Mike or to me to question him. Besides that, Mike would have done anything to get gas in his car. Anything! "What are we waiting for?" Mike said and filled the garden hose with water. I held my thumb over the end of the hose nearest the Packard while Dave shoved the other end of the hose deep into the gas tank of the Chevy.

Mike directed me to release my thumb and water rushed out of the end of the hose. I laid it on the asphalt and we waited for the tell-tale color of gold to replace the clear cool water. We stared at the flow, knowing we could not insert the hose if water were still coming out. Everyone knows you can wreck an engine by putting water in the gas tank.

"What's taking so long?" I said.

"Who knows," answered Mike intently staring at the continuing flow which was spreading out rapidly next to the Packard.

"There must be more water in a seventy-five foot hose than I thought," I observed.

"Must be," responded Mike, still watching for the evidence that gas was beginning to flow. It still looked cool and clear.

I finally reached down and touched the steady rapid stream. I lifted the hose to my nose. "It's gas, Mike," I blurted out. "Stick the hose in the tank now."

Mike was still not convinced. Not wanting any water in his mother's gas tank, he touched the flow and smelled it for himself. "Smells like gas, all right. Let's let it run just a little more to make sure that there's no water in it."

Gas continued to spread in a widening circle as Mike waited about twenty more seconds to be sure that the hose was rinsed free of water. Both Mike and I could now smell the gas fumes that billowed unseen all around us until it was hard to breathe.

"I don't think we are supposed to be breathing gas fumes, Mike."

"Why not?"

"It kills brain cells or something like that."

"Then relax, you don't have anything to worry about!"

"I'm not kidding, Mike. This isn't good for us. I think we can get lead poisoning from breathing this stuff too." I was getting a little miffed with Mike. He wasn't taking me seriously at all with the hose or with the fumes.

"This much won't hurt us," Mike said skeptically. When he was sure that he had five or six gallons of gas in the Packard's tank he called out to Dave to pull out his end of the hose. In no time at all the remainder of the gas from the hose finished its journey from the Chevy to the Packard. That indicated to me that gas had been running out of the hose long before either of us had noticed it—even much longer than we had imagined.

The huge pool next to the Packard took on an ominous appearance as we stared at it. "Mike, you'd better not light a match anywhere near that pool. It's got to be mostly gas," I cautioned.

Mike nodded now, considering the strong possibility that he had waited far too long to put the hose in the gas tank. He reached down to touch the asphalt. It was soft. The gasoline was dissolving it. The asphalt was turning into black mush and was sure to leave a black stain in the shape of a fifteen by twenty foot egg.

"Holy cow!" Mike yelled, "We're wrecking the street. Help me push the Packard back in the garage." Dave and I pushed with all our strength while Mike sat behind the steering wheel. When it was parked he jumped out, slamming the garage door behind him. He ran to the street where he discovered that the asphalt looked worse than ever.

"What a mess," Mike moaned. He looked at me. "Did you know gasoline could do this to asphalt?"

"No way, I just knew about the brain stuff and lead. What are you going to do?"

"It's already soaked in so we can't wash it away. I don't know what to do," Mike said in quiet desperation.

Dave scratched his still uncombed hair. "Couldn't be that much gas," he said. "Maybe you could just light it and it would burn out of the asphalt like kerosene out of a lantern."

Mike stared at the mushy asphalt and agreed. "Way I see it, it's the only shot I got. It's worth a try." Mike reached into his pocket and pulled out a pack of matches. We looked at each other, shrugged and Mike struck the match.

It was like an explosion, a holocaust.

Mike hadn't even thrown the match. The fumes were apparently all around us. We were blown off of our feet onto the pavement. For a brief second we were all engulfed in the flames. The heat was so intense, we had to crawl backwards immediately to keep from being toasted. Then the fire confined itself to the fifteen by twenty foot circle in the asphalt. The pillar of fire soared twenty feet in the air, screaming as it sucked air to satisfy its lust to burn. I'm sure that the black smoke rising into the late morning sky could be seen for miles.

When we were safely away from the lake of fire roaring before us, Mike finally spoke. "Good idea, Dave," but you could tell he didn't mean it.

I became aware that I felt singed. My face was hot like

when you get real sunburned. I felt my face and felt stubble where eyebrows used to be. My hair felt like steel wool, all kinky and dry as a bone. Then I glanced at Mike and Dave, who were still staring at the fire. They looked like characters from a roadrunner cartoon and I guessed I did too. Their eyebrows were all but gone and their heads were black stubble and smoking. Our tee shirts had holes burned in them. We looked like the Smokey the Bear fan club re-enacting his inspirational moment.

I suddenly became aware of the blare of sirens. "Hey guys, we have to get out of here. I think they might figure out who did this."

Mike and Dave turned to me, shocked at my appearance. "Guess what guys, you look just like me or worse," I said. We ran for Dave's house and stood in his living room arguing about what to do.

My own position was that there was no need for all of us to take the rap. "Mike, let's face it. This was your idea—the joy ride, the gas, the whole banana. I'd kind of like to keep out of this deal, if it's all the same to you. I'm going to have a hard enough time explaining how I look to my folks as it is. So maybe you should go out and confess. Whoever called the police and fire departments is a neighbor, so you're had any way you look at it. But they probably don't know me. Dave, you're on your own, but I don't think it looks too good for you either."

Dave looked at Mike and said, "We better get out there. It will probably go better for us if we give ourselves up." They looked at me in a helpless sort of way and then walked out the door. I didn't feel right staring at the closed door and ran to join my friends. When I had caught up to them, Mike said, "You don't need to do this." I said, "We're friends. Friends stick together." Mike raised where his eyebrows used to be and smiled his thanks.

When we got outside the fire captain walked up to us and said, "You boys wouldn't know anything about this, would you?" We all nodded in unison. Mike told him the whole story, even his plans for the joy ride. Meanwhile the firemen finished putting out the last of the fire. The pavement was buckled, bubbled, burnt, and dark black. There was one more thing we hadn't noticed before. The fire had burnt to a crisp two adult Ficus trees. All their leaves were wilted and burned on the street side. They died completely in a few days.

Now I thought we looked pretty funny. Had I been a fireman or a policeman, I would have at least smiled at the charred remains of adolescent humility that stood before me. But these guys did not. I suppose they had seen so many horrible things that fire can do that they must have seen us as lucky idiots. Both the fire captain and the policeman just shook their heads as they took notes on Mike's story of calculated deception and bungling.

I felt like I had just starred in a Laurel and Hardy or Three Stooges movie. Mike took full responsibility for the whole affair, and his family paid for the repair of the pavement and the replacement of the trees. He was punished pretty severely but I can't remember how. I just got a lecture from my dad which ended with, "I guess all's well that ends well. Don't do it again. You'll be pushing your luck." Dave as I remember was comforted and probably cautioned about hanging around with riffraff like Mike and me.

We did not enjoy the company of our peers for about a month. Without eyebrows we didn't fit in anyway, and since the singed condition of our hair was not compelling to the ladies, we avoided them. We just formed our own subculture: cool nerds.

The obvious lesson of our escapade was, "Be sure your sins will find you out." Apparently neither Mike nor I learned it because we both continued to do those kinds of things for a long time. I'm not sure why that particular lesson was so hard to learn. I would discover later on that I needed a strength beyond my own to refrain from yielding to foolishness. I was addicted to foolishness—fun for the sake of fun.

While that terrible incident didn't keep me from foolishness, it did remind me of the value of friendship.

I wouldn't have liked remembering that story if it had ended with my looking out of Dave's window at my friends taking the rap by themselves. I would have felt like a fink, or a rat fink as Steve Allen used to say.

A bond already existed between Mike and me before I volunteered to face the firemen and the policemen with him. But you can be sure of this; when I did choose to stand by his side, that bond of friendship grew stronger. He was my friend, my best friend at the time. I could not do less than stand by him and feel good about the quality of my friendship. I knew in my heart that Mike wouldn't hesitate to do the same thing for me. I also knew it wouldn't have taken a second thought for him to walk out that door to be by my side.

It takes real love to stand by someone when you don't have to. It takes more love when you know you don't deserve to get in trouble with them. This was truly one of a handful of times in my own life when I felt in a small way the quality of love that brought the Lord Jesus to stand by me when he didn't have to. He didn't deserve any rap, especially mine, but he took it because he considered me one of his best friends. I don't know why he did. I didn't deserve his friendship. But because of my friendships and that day I stood with Mike, I understand in a small way that it somehow brought Jesus joy to love me and be my friend.

14

Did You Ever Have Two of Those Days?

I FELL IN LOVE A LOT WHEN I WAS YOUNG. I seemed to be prone to it. In retrospect I think it would have been easier to be accident prone. No matter what accident you name, a broken heart can cause more pain. In my young flings I was usually the one that got the "boot," the "tootle loo," the "later, Jack."

I got hurt more often than not and found the old saying to be very true; "It's puppy love that leads to a dog's life." But on the other hand, "Better to have loved and lost than never to have loved at all." I'm glad that I finally met Carol, my bride of twenty-seven years now, because she has guarded my heart and nurtured it with no intention of breaking it again.

But that wasn't true of Ruthy Lewis.

I met Ruthy on a rooters' bus. We were both sophomores at Muir High School in Pasadena and our team was really something that year. It was the in thing to travel with the team, so I attended almost every away game. I jumped onto the bus with my friend Mike Meagher and we made our way toward the back of the bus where you could horse around more without bugging the bus driver.

TWITTERPATED

As I slid across the seat I looked over my shoulder to see who was in back of us. Bad mistake. I locked eyes with a petite brown-haired beauty with piercing hazel-green eyes. She smiled at me.

Did you ever see that scene in Bambi where Thumper, Flower, and Bambi all get "twitterpated" when they look at their sweethearts for the first time? Well, that's what I must have looked like. I could barely manage a smile, I was so smitten. I was smote, the next stage worse than smitten.

She said, "Hi, I'm Ruthy Lewis. This is my best friend, Donna Banks. What's your names?"

Just for a second I forgot, but did manage to keep from drooling or saying, "Duh," or something more primal. Mike spoke up for us, saying, "I'm Mike Meagher and this is my friend, Gary Richmond." I managed a smile and a nod.

"Don't you just love the rooters' bus?" exploded Ruthy, directing her comment to me again.

I felt like I looked red. I felt crimson. "It's great," I agreed. "We have a great team this year. The games have been real exciting," I added as I stared into two of the prettiest eyes I had ever seen up to that point of my life. Ruthy's girlfriend was nice, even cute, but she wasn't the knockout Ruthy was. I decided right away that if this was a real good night, Mike would be sitting next to Donna Banks on the way home. I would be next to Ruthy.

It was a real good night and that's exactly how we came home. I found my tongue at some point that night and we talked about everything we could fit in from 4:30 p.m. to 11:30 p.m. I found out she was a "La Canada" girl. Let me explain. Muir High School was made up of more than four thousand students from three cities: Altadena, Pasadena, and La Canada.

If you came from Altadena or Pasadena, the next question was what part, because both cities fed in students from rich, poor, and middle-class neighborhoods. If you came from La Canada you had three possible origins also: rich, real rich, and extremely wealthy. As it turned out Ruthy was real rich. I know because I got Mike Meagher to drive me by her house that next day.

I kind of felt like the carriage had turned into a pumpkin and I would just have a nice memory of a pretty, rich girl being real nice to me on a rooters' bus. I didn't even try to look her up afterwards, figuring that a nice girl like her could do a whole lot better than me, and she ought to.

The funny thing was that her best friend Donna told me later that week that Ruthy was kind of hurt that I hadn't followed up on her willingness to give me her address and phone number. I felt ten feet tall, maybe twenty, and could hardly wait to call her after school.

When Ruthy answered the phone, I was in heaven. She sounded excited to hear from me. I couldn't believe it.

Ruthy blurted right out, "Why didn't you call me, Gary? I gave you my phone number because I wanted you to have it. You don't think I'm the kind of girl that gives her phone number out to every Manny, Moe, and Jack? I gave it to you because I had a good time last Saturday night."

I wasn't sure what to say so I decided on the truth. "I know you're not the kind of girl that would do anything wrong. To tell you the truth I didn't feel good enough for you. I think you're the nicest girl I ever met and for sure the cutest." I meant that at the time. I was really smitten.

Ruthy sighed. "Those are the nicest things anybody has ever said to me. Tell me some more please." She sort of made things easy. "Well, to tell you the truth, you have the prettiest eyes I have ever seen in my life and I haven't been able to stop thinking about you for five minutes in a row since we left each other Saturday night. I liked the way you laughed at my jokes and…"

"That's because you're so funny, silly."

"I think you have pretty hair and your perfume drove me crazy all night. Can that be enough for now?"

"Yes, and I loved it. Well… aren't you going to ask me out? If you think I'm so great, you probably want to ask me out, don't you?"

"Sure. A guy would have to be a jerk not to want to be with you."

"When, where, and what shall I wear?"

"I don't know yet. Mike drives, but I won't be getting my license for a while yet. Maybe he'd like to take Donna out and we could double date."

"Sounds great. When can you let me know so I can look forward to it?"

"I'll call Mike right now. He liked Donna and got her number, but I don't know if he's called her yet."

"I know."

"You do? How?"

"Donna's my best friend. We don't have any secrets."

"Has he?"

"Has he what?"

"Ruthy!"

"Called her?"

"Uh huh."

"Yes. And he's waiting for you to call me and set up a double date."

"How did you know I'd call?"

"I didn't for sure. But Donna said you looked like you might call me after school."

"She kind of encouraged me."

"I told her to."

"You did? I'm really glad you did. I haven't felt this great in a long time."

"Why not?"

"It's hard to put into words but I sort of feel like you're like a princess and well, like I'm a..."

"Prince?"

"Frog."

"That's so sweet. But I don't want you to feel like that from now on."

"It feels okay. I feel pretty special right now. I better call Mike and see what we'll be doing. He's got the wheels. I'll call you back as soon as I know what's going on. And Ruthy, thank you."

"For what?"

"Making me feel a little bit less like a frog."

"I told you not to..."

"Can't help it. See you later."

I couldn't call Mike fast enough. We made arrangements to go out to eat at Bob's Big Boy Hamburgers and to a real romantic show. That night the radio was playing Johnny Mathis' biggest hit, "Misty." That became our song. The night was a roaring success and in three weeks we were going steady.

THE OTHER SIDE OF THE TRACKS

Then came the night I was dreading—the night that I met Ruthy's parents. If I were as rich as the Lewis' I wouldn't want my daughter to be dating a guy like me from the other side of the tracks. I dressed as nicely as I could and practiced yes ma'am, yes sir, please, and thank you very much most of the day.

When I got to the door I was cordially greeted by her father who was wearing a business suit with his tie loosened. He was a major vice president of some company who was clearly used to meeting and entertaining people. I was glad Mike and Donna were with me.

We were invited to sit down on the couch and were joined by Mrs. Lewis who was very society. She floated in gracefully and greeted us kindly. I could tell that both of them were sizing me up. The conversation started right off where I hoped it wouldn't. "So Gary, tell us a little about yourself," said Mrs. Lewis with genuine vested interest.

I didn't have the slightest clue as to what to say. I wasn't very impressive. The truth would have sounded a bit like this: "I'm from one of the least expensive neighborhoods in Altadena. My mother is in and out of mental institutions—she's home right now. My dad is real blue collar. He makes an honest buck plastering houses and does pretty good because he works a lot of overtime and has a good union. I get mostly bad grades because I don't give a rip, and my goal in life is to be a jazz bassist in a modern jazz band. I would kill for your daughter if she asked me to because I worship the ground she walks on and I don't have the slightest clue why she likes me either."

But I couldn't say all that! So I said, "I'm a sophomore, like Ruthy, and I live in Altadena almost directly east of you. (That left in doubt whether I was rich or poor.) Mike is my best friend and I like music, especially jazz, a whole lot."

Ruthy chimed in, "Gary plays in the orchestra under the direction of Mr. Brown. He's great. He's in a great band and they've played the Gas Lantern on Balboa Island."

"Do you like classical music, Gary?" asked Mrs. Lewis.

Oh, how I wanted to impress her and him too. "I like Bach and Beethoven and Strauss. I like the 'Grand Canyon Suite,' 'Clare De Lune,' and 'The Nutcracker Suite.' But I must confess I like jazz a bit more."

Ruthy chimed in again and I must confess I was glad of the help. "Gary played in the talent assembly. He played back up—that's the expression isn't it?—for a song from *Porgy and Bess*. It was wonderful. I never thought the school would stop clapping."

Then Ruthy's dad asked the worst possible question. "So how are the grades? You headed toward college?"

Now they had me. "Well, there is room for improvement but I am working at it." Mike threw in that I was really smart and read every book I could get my hands on. (Mostly novels and only rarely a classic.)

"What does your father do?" continued Mrs. Lewis.

"He builds houses and does room additions." I made him sound like a contractor because at the time I didn't know any better and was still struggling with the idea that my dad came home dirty every night and had thick calloused hands from spreading plaster by the ton.

"What does your father do, Mike?" asked Mr. Lewis mercifully. The interview was over for me, thank God, even though I didn't know him yet.

"He is a business man. He invests in inventions and markets them. He owns the patent on the kitchen sink faucet where you don't have two handles but the temperature is controlled by just one handle. I can see from here you have one of his handles." They did on their kitchen sink.

"He must be very successful," said Mr. Lewis.

"He's very successful and the best part about it is he's really nice to everybody. He's a neat guy," I added to keep the focus on Mike for a while. They were intrigued to know how Mike's dad had secured the patent and I didn't have to answer any more questions before we left for our date.

The heat was off, but to tell you the truth, I knew I didn't really fit in with Ruthy's family. I knew way down deep I was just a fad, a rich girl's toy. Oh, she loved me in her own way, like Snow White loved Grumpy, Happy, or Doc. I was a novelty, a jazz musician, a comedian. Ruthy's love for me was different in every way than my love for her.

I worshiped the ground she walked on. Thought of her every time a love song played on the radio. I dreamed about Ruthy and sometimes I just sat and wrote her name in different styles. I carved our names in a tree and even tried to make up love songs about her. That was hard because toothy and youthy were the only words I could think of that rhymed with Ruthy. I bought her gifts, flowers, and candy. Pretty good for a poor boy from the other side of the tracks.

We had some good times, but she began to lose interest. I could feel it, but refused to admit it. I just bought more gifts, told more jokes, dressed better, and tried hard to water a wilting flower. The six months we had gone together had been the best time of my life. I didn't want anything to change or end.

But it was ending. Ruthy's kisses were not as long and I could often tell she had something she would rather be doing than talking to me on the phone. Sometimes when we were together I felt her mind was somewhere else. I would ask her what was wrong and she'd try harder to have a good time but it wasn't the same. The fire was barely embers, but I didn't want to admit it.

Ruthy was more mature than I was. She knew it was over and wanted to preserve our friendship but nothing else. I was invited over for supper, the last supper. I think her mother knew what was happening. She seemed gracious, polite, and very proper, but there was an elusive something more. She seemed somehow relieved and relaxed in a different way. That should have been a clue but I didn't want any evidence. I didn't want to see any handwriting on the wall.

BREAKING UP IS HARD TO DO

The dinner was very good, better than anything I would ever get at home. I'm glad I didn't know it was my last meal there. Ruthy was pleasant, but a little distant, a little business-like and that seemed odd. She was no longer the brash, available little coquette. Her mother excused herself and Ruthy and I sat on the couch in the living room. She turned toward me so that I wouldn't put my arm around her and looked down as she began.

"Gary, we've had a great six months. Nobody has ever been as nice to me as you have. When we started going steady I couldn't imagine that I would ever stop loving you as a sweetheart, but I have."

"Ruthy?" I gasped. "I..."

"No, let me finish, Gary. This is hard for me because I feel guilty. If I could make myself keep loving you like I did, I would because you're so nice, but I can't. I guess this kind of love just happens and keeps happening if it's meant to be. I know you're not ready to break up, but I have to. I want to stay friends."

"Is there another guy?" I asked.

"No, not really, but one of the signs that it was time to break up was that I started to think, 'Gee it would be fun to go out with him or him.' Then I would catch myself and say I have to be loyal to Gary, we're going steady. But there have been guys that have asked me, and I would have said yes if we hadn't been going together."

I couldn't think of anything to say. Ruthy had closed every door. I don't know where people go to school to learn to break up but she must have gone to Harvard. Except you know what? No matter how well someone is rejected, it still hurts.

She held my hand and said, "Don't you want to say something?"

"What's there to say? We had some pretty good times. I don't want them to end, but you do. It takes two people to want to make it and we don't have two and your vote is bigger than mine. You broke up with me in a nice way, dinner and all."

"I still want to be friends," she said sincerely.

"Well, I couldn't hate you or anything like that but I don't think we'll be hanging out much. I couldn't... it would be too.... I think it's nice when people can stay friends but..."

"You mean you don't even want to stay friends?" she asked as though that was beyond her understanding.

"You know how I like to eat hot fudge sundaes at Bob's Big Boy?"

"Yes."

"You would be a hot fudge sundae that I had tasted but couldn't eat. Only I'd want you about a thousand times more than a hot fudge sundae from anywhere. Do you know what I mean? I can't help wanting you to be my girlfriend anymore than you could make yourself like me again."

"I like you. You're one of my closest friends."

"Right now it hurts to hear that because you're still more than one of my best friends. You're the most important person in my life."

"I think I understand. Would you like to stay and watch television?"

"No, thank you. If you don't mind I'll just call my dad and see if he can pick me up."

"Gary, you don't have to go."

"Yes, I do."

I called my dad and he said, "Seems a bit early, Gary. I'm surprised to hear from you."

"I know, Dad, but we're all done and if it's okay I'd like you to come and get me." It was fine with him because it meant he could go to bed earlier and he was always pretty tired on Friday nights. He would be there in fifteen minutes.

I wanted to remember my manners so I thanked Mrs. Lewis for the really nice dinner and she smiled an understanding smile like she knew why I was leaving early. Ruthy followed me out the front door and I told her she didn't have to wait with me and she said she knew that. I didn't say anything more because I was afraid if I talked much I'd cry or beg or say something bitter and I wanted to leave with my dignity intact.

Even though I was poor, I was proud after a fashion and knew what a man should do to keep his honor. Besides, Ruthy couldn't help how she felt. We sat silently and she leaned her head against my shoulder. Her hair smelled of shampoo, and her perfume surrounded me for the very last time. She was crying.

"Why are you crying, Ruthy?"

"Because I know you're hurting, and I don't like hurting someone I care deeply about."

"I know."

"Do you want to kiss me goodnight?"

"Goodbye?"

"Yes."

We kissed in the moonlight, a bittersweet farewell. It was a nice note to end on. My dad arrived in our little Nash Rambler and I climbed in after Ruthy squeezed my hand. I was aware that her perfume had rubbed off onto my shirt and I closed my eyes and breathed it in. Her smell was the next thing to being with her, but it also reminded me of how things were. The pain began to wash over me. Time would have to do its healing work.

My dad broke the silence. "You want to talk about it, son?"

"Isn't too much to say, Dad. Ruthy dumped me tonight. She did it in a nice way, but that doesn't make me feel much better about it. I kind of wish we'd argued or something."

My dad was quiet for a few minutes, then he said, "Nothing much I could say right now would make you feel better, but if I could I would. Gary, if they don't make you happy they're not meant for you."

That was true and it was something Ruthy had discovered before I did. We rode about a mile farther and my dad said one more thing. "Try to remember this, son. She's not the only tin can in the dump!" They turned out to be the last words he would ever say to me in this life.

He was looking straight ahead and smiling. I smiled too. He had said it to make me feel better, kind of a slam on Ruthy for dumping me. I have never forgotten those words. I hope my last words will cheer someone up a little.

When we got out of the car Dad just squeezed my arm and smiled with deep concern and understanding. He knew what it was to hurt this way. Then we went to bed. It took me awhile to fall asleep. I ached like I had never ached before. I held my shirt close to my cheek and smelled Ruthy's perfume until the wondrous vapors blended with dreams that would never be fulfilled.

A SEVERE MERCY

I woke up feeling sorry for myself. But nothing ever seems to adversely affect my appetite. In fact everything makes me hungry. So I got up and wandered into the dining room. My dad was standing across the partition between the dining room and living room, fixing an electric socket he had removed from the wall. He looked pale and was perspiring, which was unusual for a task that required so little effort. My mother smiled sympathetically like she had been told about Ruthy and me.

I walked into the kitchen and fixed myself a bowl of Wheaties, the breakfast of champions. Maybe that would help, I thought. I sat down at the dining room table and took a bite. I looked up to see my dad holding the electric socket about chest high. His hands were shaking and he looked as though he was scared to death. Then his eyes closed and he dropped to the floor. Both my mother and I were by his side in three seconds.

My mother gently slapped his cheeks and said, "Honey, what's wrong? Honey, say something!" She sat down on the floor and pulled his head and shoulders up onto her lap and said, "Walter Richmond, don't you leave me. Gary! For God's sake call an ambulance, now."

I ran for the phone and my hands were shaking violently. I couldn't think what to do so I dialed operator. When she answered I said, "We need help, my dad may be dying. We need an ambulance right away."

She had a kind and very calm voice. "What's your name and address, please?" I gave it to her and she sweetly asked me to hold the line. I could hear her speaking to St. Luke Hospital in the background, requesting an ambulance, and felt a little better. She came back on the line and said, "Gary, they're on their way. I hope your father will be okay. Do you want me to stay on the line?"

"No, thank you, operator." She wished me luck. My father's eyes were open and his pupils were fixed and dilated. If I had known those symptoms, I would have been more afraid than I was. My mother was rocking him back and forth in her lap and running her fingers through his curly hair.

Normally, I was not a God-fearing person. I didn't think of him much at all most of the time, and when I did, it wasn't serious. My most recent conversation regarding God was with my brother Steve, who had begun to attend the Assembly of God Church in Pasadena. I accused him of being a "goody, goody." He said it wouldn't hurt me any to come to church, but I told him I didn't need any of that God stuff and was doing fine without him. My brother shrugged his shoulders and dropped the subject.

Suddenly I knew that if anything good was going to happen in this situation, God would have to do it. Figuring I had nothing to lose and my father's life to gain, I opened a conversation with God. "God, you don't owe me anything but my dad's a good man and he needs you. I'll go to church, study hard, stop swearing, and anything else you would want me to do if you'll just let my dad live. Please let him live. We need him. My mom couldn't make it without him. God, please let him live. Amen."

I just leaned helplessly against the partition and looked down at my dad. I could see that he was breathing. His eyes were open and he never blinked. I closed my eyes and again begged God to not let him die. Where was the ambulance? I thought. I could hear the siren in the distance. The antique clock was ticking loudly and the seconds seemed so long.

The ambulance arrived about fifteen minutes after we had called. I guided them into the house. They quickly put oxygen over my dad's face and loaded him into the ambulance. My mother jumped in the back and they sped off to St. Luke Hospital.

I waited for nearly an hour with no news. Then I called my Uncle Bill, who was my idol, and he and my Aunt Patty said they would come over as soon as possible. They loved my dad and sounded terrified at the thought that we might be losing him.

I sat and waited, in tears and on the verge of panic. After thirty more minutes, a car pulled up to our house and dropped off my mother. Our eyes met as she came in the door. Her first words were, "My God, Gary! Whatever is to become of you? I'm too weak to keep you under control, and we've lost your father. He's gone. He won't be coming home anymore."

I was stunned. This wasn't possible. My dad was a rock, invincible. He was strong as an ox and never lost a day's work to sickness. He couldn't do that to me, to us. My mother was right. Whatever would become of me? I wasn't that good a kid and could run over my mother like a steamroller.

Moments before we were a family. Now I didn't know what we were anymore. A weak-natured, alcoholic mom. A strong-willed child who liked living on the edge. An older brother who couldn't understand me because we were so totally different. Somehow my dad had tied us all together and made it work. Now what?

When my uncle and aunt arrived, it helped me feel less like the whole world had turned upside down. But the time came when they had to go home, leaving the house silent except for the sobbing of my mother.

Nothing made any sense. I needed Ruthy.

I walked to the Mobil gas station and called her. I felt better just hearing her voice answer the phone. "Ruthy, my dad died today. He died of a heart attack and we didn't even know he had any problems. Do you mind talking to me?"

"No, Gary, I don't mind. Gary, how can I tell you how sorry I am?"

"Thanks. I just needed to talk with someone. Are you sure you don't mind?"

"No. Go ahead," she said sweetly.

"Ruthy, do you think you could like wait a little while longer to break up with me? I need you. I need someone to feel close to right now."

There was silence on the other end of the line.

"Ruthy?"

"I'm here. Gary, I can't tell you how bad I feel but this doesn't change things for us. It wouldn't make you feel better to know it would be over again in just a little while."

"Yeah, I guess you're right. Well, it was worth a try. Ruthy, I didn't know somebody could feel this bad."

"Gary, I'm sorry. I really am."

"I have to go now. Things will get better. I love you."

I hung up the phone and laid my head against the glass door of the gas station, just staring at the pavement. I walked over to Mike Meagher's house. He was a really good friend. He helped a lot.

My father was buried at North Hollywood Forest Lawn on

January 13, 1960. His best friends were there and he had a lot of them. You know what I remember most about the funeral? How many people said, "Your dad was a good man, a man of his word. We'll miss him." At the family reception afterward, a lot of people said, "If your dad said he'd do something, that was money in the bank. He'd do it when he said he'd do it and die before he'd break his word."

All anyone ever needed from him was a handshake, more powerful than any contract ever written. My father was a man of his word. And he was so much more. He was a man's man. He was strong from hard, honest work. He was a great dad. And he was the most loyal husband I have ever known. Dad stuck by my mom like glue during the worst times of her life. He knew firsthand the deeper meaning of "for better or for worse."

God was creating a vacuum in my life—a great big empty hole where Ruthy used to be and a bigger one where my father used to be. These events were part of a severe mercy for me. God was big enough to fill the emptiness to over-flowing, but when the crisis was over, I didn't feel like I needed him anymore.

Anyway, things couldn't get worse. But they did.

15

A Long Night's Journey

MY JUNIOR YEAR IN HIGH SCHOOL was the most eventful year of my life. Your sixteenth year is supposed to be filled with hope for a bright future, true loves, a sense of impending adulthood, and of course, your driver's license. I got all those things and a basket full of others I didn't want.

The worst day of my life came on January 10, 1960, when my dad died of a heart attack in my mother's arms while I looked on—terrified and helpless. By the middle of March, it was clear that life was going to go on one way or another without my dad. But my mother wasn't doing very well. The grieving process was eating her alive. She cried every night. My room was next to hers and when she cried I couldn't sleep.

I couldn't cry either, but I figured Mom was crying enough for the whole family. I felt like I ought to cry, and to this day I'm not sure why I didn't. My theory is that I was afraid that my life would fall apart if I didn't act like I thought a man ought to act in these circumstances. So I stuffed my feelings and weathered the storm.

Mother became very actively alcoholic and brought home men she would pick up in bars. I hated them and her for her disloyalty to my father. Then she began to buy wine at a local liquor store and drink all day and night at our kitchen table. She just stared out the window at our neighbor's house and smoked pack after pack of cigarettes. Her teary eyes reflected a deep, unresolved pain. We never talked about feelings in our home even before my dad died, so I didn't ask my mother how she was doing or what she was feeling. My mother, brother, and I were all going it alone. It was so sad because we really could have helped each other. We just didn't.

I think my mother filled up with pain until she couldn't stand it any longer. Then she went on a binge. My brother was informed by phone that he was to come and get my mother. She was in the Lincoln Heights jail. She had been drunk and disorderly and was arrested, with handcuffs, fingerprinting, and all that goes with it. As the older brother, Steve had gotten stuck with this kind of duty a lot. He had been called to pick my mother up from local bars on several occasions but this event was especially humiliating.

My mother was hopelessly addicted to prescription drugs and severely alcoholic. The grief finally caught up with her. Under the weight of the guilt and her failing health, Mother had a full-blown nervous breakdown. From that day on she lived in either one of California's state mental institutions or with her parents until her mother died of cancer.

LOOKING BACK

When I was eight years old I would have told you that I lived in a normal, happy family—the "Leave It to Beaver" kind with a blue collar dad. My father and mother got along fine and seemed to like me most of the time. We went to visit my grandparents a lot, which I loved because they loved to spoil me rotten. My grandparents and great-grandparents lived next door to one another in a duplex. When I sensed that one set was tired of adoring and spoiling me, I would just go next door and let the other set take their turn. I loved feeling like a little prince. Life was grand.

Both grandmothers were terrific cooks. In the tradition of southern cooking, there was lots and lots of fried chicken, mashed potatoes, and gravy. And both grandfathers were great storytellers. Pap, my grandfather, had been a professional baseball player and had actually played against the great Babe Ruth. He was a direct descendent of Mad Anthony Wayne, a Revolutionary War general. Pap never ran out of stories, which he always told with exaggerated enthusiasm. He took me everywhere he went and bragged about me to all of his friends.

So you can imagine I was a pretty happy kid in those days. Who wouldn't be?

Then things began to change. My mother became depressed and spent hours crying in her room. She stopped laughing and singing. The worst part was she stopped having time for me and my brother. My dad tried to tell me that I hadn't done anything wrong but somehow I found myself wondering if I was to blame for making her so unhappy.

As it turned out my mother was sad because she was losing the use of her legs. She was finding it harder and harder to walk. The doctor could find no reason for her symptoms. He told her that medical science had no more to offer her, that she wasn't walking because she didn't want to walk. He called it hysterical paralysis and advised my mother and father to see a psychiatrist.

The psychiatrist supported the physician's diagnoses. My mother really believed there was something physically wrong, but reluctantly began the psychiatric process that cost countless thousands of dollars. It ultimately cost my father his life, because he worked himself to death paying for what turned out to be a mistaken diagnoses—a bad mistake that may have cost my mother's life as well.

The truth was discovered seventeen years later. My mother's spinal cord had been scarred by a spinal injection administered during one of her two Cesarean sections. The scar tissue had grown dramatically and choked off the spinal cord in such a way that her brain could not send messages to her legs. The original radiologist had missed seeing the thickened tissue when her back had been x-rayed.

Mother's walking failed slowly and was worse on some days than on others. When feeling in her legs returned some days, her hopes would be raised and her eyes would brighten. Then the next day it was everything she could do to get out of a chair. Depression would set in, the tears would flow, and a little bit more light would disappear from her eyes. Mom started drinking heavily to feel better by feeling nothing.

My father worked forty exhausting hours a week and began remodeling houses on the weekends to pay the obscenely large hourly charges made by the psychiatrist, a skinny, balding man with thick horn-rimmed glasses. He asked one probing personal question after another. He told my mother that she *could* walk, that she was in denial about some hidden trauma that caused her to fear facing life. There was a catch-22 about the whole thing. My mother needed love and understanding more than anything. But the person who best offered it was forced to work every available hour to cover the expenses of a man who was making things worse.

Three years passed and things got worse. My mother had a nervous breakdown, explained to me only as, "Gary, she just can't handle being home." That confirmed my suspicion that I was partly to blame for my mother's condition. She was hospitalized at Camarillo State Mental Hospital about seventy miles from our home, which meant long hours of driving every week so that we could see my mother at the mental institution.

We went almost every weekend for several months and I resented it. It was not the way weekends should be spent by a nine-year-old boy. But that's the way it was. I asked my dad how he could stand it and why we didn't just stop going.

He looked at me square on and said, "Son, life deals everybody a different hand. This is the hand we been dealt, and this is the hand we're going to play. That's my wife in there and that's your mother. She needs us and we're going to be there for her no matter what."

My dad often used poker language to talk about life. Long before Kenny Rogers sang "The Gambler," my dad was saying, "You got to know when to hold them and know when to fold them, know when to walk away and know when to run." He knew in his heart that to walk away from my mother would be a great betrayal of his promise to stand by her in sickness and in health, for better or for worse, as long as they both shall live.

We never knew how we would find my mother when we visited. Sometimes she would be okay. Other times she would be withdrawn and hardly speak a word. Sometimes she would beg my father to get her out and would cry for four straight hours. On one visit we would find Mom wearing makeup with her hair combed; the next she would be unkempt with no makeup and wearing a wrinkled dress.

I probably would not have gone if my father had not made me. I'm so glad he did now. I would have had to live with the shame of abandoning my mother were it not for his own sense of duty and right.

The patients of that particular establishment were weird, and my mother even at her worst didn't seem to fit in. I saw men running around grabbing at the air as if they were chasing butterflies. Other people held long involved conversations with themselves as if they were two people. They even laughed at their own jokes when it seemed to them appropriate. Hostile people would come and threaten us with loud invictives and would spit and drool. All of us would go home exhausted from these visits.

At some point in her therapy, someone thought that shock treatments would benefit my mother. From the day of her first one she wanted out. Funny thing was she seemed to get better and they finally did let her out. But it wouldn't be too long before she would be back again. Mom just couldn't handle life on the outside, even the best of it.

Three years passed and even my closest friends didn't know all of this was going on. I figured that if anyone knew that my mother was in a mental institution, they would wonder if I was crazy too. Becoming crazy and unable to function became one of my greatest fears. If it could happen to my mother, it could possibly happen to me. I still think about that in my most private of moments and shudder.

Those closest to me think I am crazy and don't know it. I suppose that's true about most if not all crazy people. They think they're normal and everyone else is crazy. So I think of myself as a little to the right or left of center. Then I know I'm okay because a crazy person wouldn't think that. You know what I mean? If you're pretty sure you're not crazy, I'd be a little worried if I were you.

Anyway, things seemed to get better during my twelfth year. My mother was walking, a little stiff-legged, but she was walking. We were all more optimistic that whatever had been plaguing her mind was relenting. Maybe our lives would become normal or at least more like they had been before. That didn't happen. Things got worse.

SUICIDE

It was a hot September afternoon, and summer lingered like an unwanted house guest that had worn out its welcome by several weeks. School had started, and the adjustment from bare feet to shoes and lazy days to homework gave rise to rampant self-pity among all us kids. But we didn't get a drop of sympathy from adults—who must have forgotten how it was to be kids.

I just couldn't convince anybody that wearing shoes was a serious problem, with the exception of my skin doctor. I had an early case of acne and saw a dermatologist just after school started. That day my feet were bothering me, and he noticed I was limping a bit. He said, "What's wrong, son? You're limping."

"It's nothing, sir," I said. "Just a blister from trying to get used to shoes again after the summer."

My dermatologist was a little cranky. He snapped out, "Don't you tell me it's nothing, son. It's something all right. One of the doctors over at the hospital lost his son to a blister that began on his heel. His son was just like you. Said it was nothing. But it got infected, turned into gangrene, got out of control, and took him from us forever. Don't you tell me it's nothing. Take off your shoes."

The doctor studied my smallish blister and then poured iodine all over it. It burned like fire. When I asked him why iodine burned so bad, he said, "When the iodine hits the germs, they know they are dying and they take one last bite out of you as an act of revenge, and it hurts, don't it? But it's our sign that the little beggars are dying."

Then he winked at my mother and smiled at me. Moments like that made me occasionally wonder if adults were in a secret plot to help each other get back at hard-to-raise kids.

The doctor spent more time looking at my foot than my face, probably because he didn't know anybody that had died from acne. I didn't want to think it was because my foot was considerably more handsome than my face. But girls were going to be looking at my face, not my foot, and I was just beginning to be really concerned what they thought. All he did was to tell me to wash my face daily and use a new product called Clear-a-sil—a cream as much like makeup as medicine. It made a bold statement loud and clear, "I have pimples," and never cleared up much of anything.

During one of those last lingering days of September, I came home after school expecting to see my mother sitting at the kitchen table as usual, smoking a Kool cigarette and drinking a glass of cheap wine. She was not there. When I called out, the house just swallowed up my words and kept them to itself. I called out again with the same result.

Something was wrong. My mother never went anywhere by herself, not even on the bus. She was always home. She didn't have any close friends, and her parents lived thirty-five miles away, so she just stayed home and waited for us to get home. That's all she asked for. Other than when she had been hospitalized, she was always at that table when I came in the door. But not today. It was eerie.

I put down my books and looked out the back door to see if she was outside. I walked into the hallway. "Mom?" Again the words were swallowed by the silence.

Then I became aware of a smell—a sickeningly sweet smell unlike anything I had ever smelled before. Its total unfamiliarity caused a sense of unexplainable panic. I found nothing in all three bedrooms. But when I stepped back into the hallway the smell was there again.

The source of the oppressive odor seemed to be the bathroom. I slowly pushed the door open and the smell billowed out, nearly gagging me. I turned on the light and stepped into a nightmare. There was blood everywhere—on the floor, splattered on the walls, on the shower curtain, on the bathtub and sink.

The horror was real, not like the movies where you know you are just seeing an illusion or a shadow of the real thing. I stumbled backward into the hallway and ran back into the living room, trying to think what to do. I fumbled through the phone directory to call my grandparents to see if they knew what had happened. As I dialed the phone I remembered my father's warning that old people can have weak hearts, so I put down the phone.

I couldn't think of anything else to do except wait, but seconds seemed like hours. Something terrible had happened and I didn't know what. Several thoughts went through my mind. Maybe a murderer came and killed my mother and took her away. Maybe my dad... no! that wasn't even possible. I buried my head in my hands and tried to think. Should I call the police? Maybe later.

Mercifully the back door opened and there stood my father. He looked tired and sad, but still strong as always. Our eyes met and I'm sure mine cried out my haunting questions.

"You see the bathroom, son?" he asked.

"Yes, Dad. What happened?"

"Your mother decided she didn't want to live anymore, and she cut her wrists hoping she'd bleed to death. If I hadn't gotten home a little early from work today she might have died. I don't know. Son, I wish you hadn't seen that bathroom. I was hoping to get it cleaned up before you got home from school. Try to forget it. Can't do you no good to think about it. Won't help nothin' so try to forget it if you can. Your mother's going to be in the hospital a while this time. They have to be sure she won't try it again."

"Dad? Did I do something wrong? Did I... ?"

"Get that thought out of your head, Gary. Your mom is lost somewhere and she just can't find her way to happiness. So far nobody really knows why she is like she is, but it doesn't have anything to do with you. God knows you're not perfect, but you're normal and a whole lot better than I was at your age."

Dad squeezed my arm and said it was going to be all right. I believed him because he never gave me any reason not to. But, way down deep, I thought it probably was my fault my mom had tried to die. I thought of myself as a bad kid.

My father cleaned up the bathroom. It looked spotless when he finished but it never smelled the same again—a daily reminder of that horror-filled afternoon. I hated that room.

Mom came home in three months. I never brought a friend home from school again for fear of what I might see. I spent more and more time over at friends' houses to get away from the reality that my home was painfully different.

To make a long story short, I am going to simply tell you where this all went. My mother continued to attempt suicide—seven times in all, involving overdoses of prescription drugs after she cut her wrists. On her seventh attempt she succeeded. I was twenty-six years old and my father had been dead for eleven years.

Pinned to my mother's chest was a simple message which was handed to me when I picked up her personal effects from the hospital. She had neatly written the note on a scrap of typewriter paper and pinned it to her flannel nightgown. It contained three words which I shall never forget: "UN-WANTED, UNNEEDED, UNLOVED."

I stared at those words for a minute with mixed emotions. I felt angry and thought, "This is just like you, Mom. You want to make others feel lousy because you couldn't put the puzzle together. You couldn't find the missing piece." Then I felt guilty and wondered what I could have done to make her feel more wanted, needed, or loved. Then I felt pity. How pitiful to have felt you had written your biography in three words. My mother must have been in terrible anguish when she penned those words. She must have been sadly alone and hopeless.

Twenty years have passed since I held that scrap of paper in my hands. I can still feel its evil texture and the curse that went with it. I know in my mind and my heart that I had been a good son. My wife and I spent every day off from work visiting her, along with her granddaughters to love her so she wouldn't feel unwanted, unneeded, or unloved. Even knowing I had done my best, there are still times when I hear whispers of anger, guilt, and pity—stirring and cutting and accusing me when I remember the note.

Thirty-five years have passed since I turned on that bathroom light. I can still smell the smell and remember the terror.

16

The First Day of the Rest of My Life

YOU DO WHAT YOU HAVE TO DO TO SURVIVE . I didn't like life without a dad or a mom. I didn't like having a twenty-year-old brother entertaining occasional fantasies about being a substitute father. Steve didn't like it any more than I did, but he must have felt responsible.

I didn't buy it. We either had occasional cross words or we didn't say much at all. I just figured we'd do the best we could to raise ourselves. My approach to life was simple when dealing with my brother. You sweat you, and I'll sweat me.

My brother had good reason to be worried about me. I was running with friends in the "early sixties" fast lane, most of whom were getting stoned on a regular basis. Some of the guys said they had tried marijuana, but I didn't believe them. I saw them drunk a lot, on beer mostly or liquor stolen from their parents.

I wanted to get drunk worse than anything. It was like a life's ambition at sixteen, but I couldn't bring myself to do it. My father had told me from the time I was twelve, "If I smell liquor on your breath, you don't even want to know what I'll do to you, young man." My dad spoke with deep conviction and was a man of his word. It would never occur to me not to believe him.

Since I'm the superstitious sort, I entertained the notion that one of two things would happen if I ever did get drunk. The strongest possibility was that my father would burst out of his casket, claw his way upward through the soil and roots, and walk to Pasadena so I could find out what he meant by, "You don't even want to know what I'd do to you if I ever smell liquor on your breath." Or else I just thought he would come back and haunt me out of a sense of responsibility.

Way down deep I didn't want to disappoint my dad. I was also afraid I'd become an alcoholic like my mother, two great uncles, my grandfather, and my father's mother. Our family was crawling with drunks, and I was pretty sure I could become one of them if I dabbled. One of Dad's favorite sayings was, "Son, don't play with fire if you don't want to get burned." He always said that when he was trying to make me see there was nothing great about getting drunk.

"You know what it is to get drunk?" he would say. "You lose your coordination, act like a jerk in front of everyone, and you are too blotto to care. That sound fun to you?" I always said, "No, sir," because I knew what was good for me.

But still it was hard not to get drunk when all of my best friends were getting drunk and telling me how boss it was and calling me square and chicken for holding back. I wanted to get fall-down, blotto drunk. I knew it wasn't a question of *if* I would, but *when* I would. It had to be a situation where my brother wouldn't find out and go out to Forest Lawn Cemetery and tell my dad, which I knew my brother would do. He had gotten a flaming case of religion in a church that campaigned against most of the things I had become pretty good at.

I was smoking about a half-pack of cigarettes a day, knew

more dirty jokes than anyone in my class, used all manner of filthy and inappropriate language, challenged teachers and authority figures, drag-raced at the Rose Bowl daily, lied when I didn't need to lie, cheated on tests to get by, and spent every weekend in Hollywood jazz clubs that would admit minors and let them stay until closing time.

THE STEREO CONTEST

My brother, Steve, had a girlfriend who was even more of a religious fanatic than he was. Beverly spent all of her free time at church, and that's all she could talk about. God this, God that—brother, what a bother! Well, she entered this contest at her church, The First Assembly of God Church in Pasadena. To win the contest you simply had to bring more visitors than anyone else to a week-long youth rally.

There was a lot at stake for those who had joined the competition. The winner would receive his or her own stereo phonograph just when they were first coming out. Bev wanted that stereo more than anything she had ever wanted in her life. I know that to be a fact because she was willing to invite *me* to add to her contest count. Normally, I would have been an embarrassment to Beverly and her family—living and talking the way I did—but what did that matter if I could help her win her own stereo phonograph? Not one other person in her crowd had one, and it was portable. My coming to her church would be a small enough price to pay to win such a grand prize.

So in an unguarded moment Bev and Steve asked me to come as a personal favor to both of them. My dad used to kid about his going to church. He used to say that if he ever went, the roof of the church would fall in on him as a punishment for all his evil deeds. I wondered for a minute if that would happen to me. I figured I was at greater risk since I had done worse things than my father.

I can't remember for sure why I said I would go. I must have had some ulterior motive. I wouldn't have gone just to be nice; at the time, I was not the least bit fond of my brother or his prissy puritanical princess. We must have struck a deal for something of benefit to me, but I have forgotten what it was. Going would not have been like me at all unless something really big was in it for me.

You know what they say about misery loving company? I talked two of my friends who were every bit as wild as I was into coming to church with me that night. "What's the big deal, you guys?" I said when I invited them. "We'll just sit there for about an hour or so, then we'll leave and go cruising. No sweat!"

My friend Mike protested, "I don't like church, man."

"You ever been?"

"No, because I don't like it."

"We're not going because we like it. We're doing it for my brother's main squeeze so she can win this stereo. Ninety minutes. How bad can it be? It will be educational, you know what I mean? Then bang, we hit Bob's Big Boy, check out the chicks, meet them if we can, cruise Colorado Boulevard, swing by the Rose Bowl and see who's drag racing and go home. It's business as usual except we do my brother's girl a favor. Come on. I'd do this for you guys and you know it." They knew it too because we were good friends. We did everything together, usually all for one and one for all.

I wore them down like I always did and they agreed to come with me. I'm not sure why I asked them when I knew that I was increasing the chances that the church roof would fall on all of us by three hundred percent. As it turned out, that night was the end of years of close friendship. One of us was to turn down a different road that night and never really look back.

Mike drove that night because he had the neatest car. His parents let him take the '53 Packard convertible—not a real teen machine but it made us look rich. We all had this idea that girls preferred rich guys to poor guys.

On this warm May night, we drove into the church parking lot with the top down and the radio blaring. We were tuned into Pasadena's favorite top-forties station, KRLA, and the Devilkings were rocking out on one of their latest hits. Several other people who were arriving came up and said hello.

I was impressed that there were so many kids my age and surprised that I didn't know even one of them. I found out most of them went to Pasadena High School, our biggest rival, but they remained friendly even when I admitted that I went to John Muir High. Since everyone had been pretty friendly, I decided that maybe the evening wasn't going to be so bad after all.

Mike and Eric were not quite as people-oriented as I was and didn't look like they were having any fun at all. I hadn't noticed, but Mike pointed out, "None of these chicks wear makeup and some of them need it pretty bad."

"Lighten up, Mike. They're pretty nice to us considering we're Muir guys. I thought some of them were pretty cute. Be nice. We'll be out of here in about ninety minutes."

"I'd like to leave now," said Mike sarcastically. Eric raised his eyebrows and smirked. He didn't want to be there either.

"Come on. Let's make the best of it," I encouraged. "Let's go inside and see if we can find my brother." We walked into the church foyer. Bev saw me and came running up to thank us for coming. We had to sign in so she could get credit for our being there.

My brother was more reserved. We have always looked a lot alike so everyone knew right away I was Steve's brother. I was pretty sure he was a little apprehensive about me being around his church friends. He was probably praying that I wouldn't tell some dirty jokes or use bad language or light up a cigarette.

Steve didn't know it but I was much too self-conscious to act up. For some reason I thought of church as God's house and didn't see any reason to get on his bad side any more than I already was.

In retrospect, I have found it odd that for sixteen years of my life I believed in God but avoided him. Perhaps I thought he would cramp my style. I was willingly ignorant of God's way of doing things, assuming that my way was more fun, exciting, and expanded. I vaguely thought of his program as a list of things you couldn't do and my program as an endless list of things I could do. I saw myself as a Tom Sawyer, Huck Finn, wild mustang sort of a guy who needed a frontier without boundaries to be happy. I was fairly sure God wanted to put me in a little box.

That's how I felt as I sat down in a pew two-thirds of the way back. My two friends had been struck silent by the unfamiliarity of the whole scene. As our eyes met Mike smirked again and shook his head. Eric just looked around the way pioneers did when they going through Indian country. It made me smile. I took some satisfaction in the thought that my two friends were more uncomfortable than I was.

To my surprise, the church pianist was playing a tune with a good beat. She wasn't Jerry Lee Lewis, but she was blowing my image of church music—certainly not the sterile, unsyncopated, bland music I had imagined I would hear.

I didn't know it at the time, but I was hearing white gospel music, a spin off of black gospel which eventually gave birth to Rock and Roll An organist joined in who was even more with it than the pianist. A guy jumped in on the harmonica and then a trumpet and trombone player began to jam with them. Finally, a tambourine was added. I kind of wished that I had my string bass because they could have used it and a drummer too. The organist was providing a lot of bass with her foot pedals and everything was moving real good. Yes, I was surprised.

I don't know just how to explain it, but I felt that it was okay for me to be there. Maybe I even felt that I belonged there in some strange way. I wasn't uncomfortable at all. For the first time in a long time, I actually felt good—and since I hadn't done anything good for a long time, I was due. I was usually so bad that I thought of going to church as a good deed. In return for doing church a favor by showing up, I was erasing a black mark from the ledger of life. I looked at Mike and Eric and saw they hadn't made the adjustment. You know how most dogs look when you give them a bath? Well, that's how they looked.

GOOD VIBES

The meeting started with a whole lot of singing. It was definitely a case of, "If you can't sing good, sing loud." Don't get me wrong. I enjoyed it. The singing wasn't stuffy, it was full of joy, and the voices were those of folks with a clear conscience.

They sang mostly about Jesus, someone I liked from a distance but didn't really know because we had never really met. I half felt that if I ever met Jesus, I would probably like him. It was just that we sort of ran in different crowds. The songs had neat titles, like "I've Got the Joy, Joy, Joy," "Drinking at the Springs of Living Water," and "Heavenly Sunshine." It was all upbeat stuff and everyone was really getting into it.

I don't know if you've ever been to a pentecostal church, but you would find it interesting to say the least. They are unencumbered by stuffy traditions and formality and seem to be free to worship in a no-holds-barred sort of way. I was entertained by the clapping and body movement. They were into singing and a good share of them were raising their hands, closing their eyes, and swaying back and forth.

When the singing stopped things got a little weird. When the kindly-looking pastor got up and began to pray, he seemed to inspire unsolicited participation. He couldn't get out a phrase without half the folks in the audience responding. It went sort of like this:

> Pastor: "Lord, we're here tonight to adore you!"
> Crowd: "Yes, Lord. Praise you, Jesus. Thank you, Jesus!"
> Pastor: "We want to be filled with your Spirit!"
> Crowd: "Fill us, Jesus. Fill us, Jesus. Fill us, Jesus!"
> Pastor: "Help us, Lord, to draw near to your blessed throne."
> Crowd: "We need you, Jesus."
> Pastor: (Now turned up a notch.) "Jesus, Jesus, Jesus, precious Jesus."
> Crowd: "Jesus, Jesus, Jesus, Jesus, Jesus!"

In addition to the prayers, some folks moaned, and some just raised their hands and said "Yes, Lord!" over and over and over. It was pretty intense, verging on spooky. I had my eyes closed, but thought I had better check on Mike and Eric to see how they were doing. They didn't have their eyes closed. In fact, I had never seen their eyes opened that wide. They looked like they were going to run.

I had seen that same facial expression on a frightened cat. The cat had run around a wall right into a big German shepherd. The dog looked ecstatic. The cat on the other hand looked as though it were receiving about twenty thousand volts of electricity. Mike and Eric looked like two cats in the middle of a convention of German Shepherds.

I jabbed Mike in the arm and smiled at him. He and Eric kept glaring at me with narrow eyes. I knew I was going to have to deliver my standard, "It wasn't that bad," talk after the meeting.

When the pastor stopped praying at the microphone, the church became strangely quiet. A very large woman dressed in black took the floor. She was wearing a large black hat with a big, white silk rose on it. She began to speak in a foreign language. I didn't see the point. She went on for about two minutes, and no sooner did she finish than a man across the room spoke like he was giving a little message from God. When he stopped the pastor composed himself behind his pulpit and began to introduce the evening speaker.

I thought the evening speaker was the part that we would all have to tough out, but I couldn't have been more wrong. The guy was hysterically funny and said things that seemed very important. By the end of his message, I had the distinct impression that someone had told him I was in the audience.

The speaker said he was sure there was someone in the audience who needed the kind of direction a father could give, someone who needed a reason to live and a purpose worth living for. He said God had made a way for those things to happen. He had sent Jesus down to make it possible. Jesus would let his Father be our Father and Jesus would give us a reason and a purpose to live. All we had to do was give him our life, ask God to forgive our sins, and ask him to come inside our heart and be the Lord of our lives.

I knew that I wanted exactly what the man was promising and I wanted it real bad. He invited those who wanted to meet Jesus to leave where they were standing and come to the altar. I was seriously considering going down. Then he said, "If you know someone here tonight who needs Christ, go lay hands on them and pray."

Guess which three guys got touched by the most hands in about ten seconds? Hands were coming from everywhere because everybody knew we needed Christ. The spell was broken. I just wanted out of there as quickly as possible, and I wasn't the only one. I could hear Eric saying, "Excuse me, I have to go now," but these folks were like gum on your shoe, very difficult to shake off.

I more or less took over and just started being firm that we had to be somewhere soon, but we were followed all the way to the car by a well meaning group of people who couldn't stand the thought of our getting away. They all looked just like a fisherman who had just lost the big one.

WILD AND CRAZY

As we drove out of the parking lot I glanced at Mike, who was driving a bit faster and jerkier than usual. He looked very angry. Mike and I had been buddies for years and I had seen him ticked off before, but not this ticked off. He looked straight ahead, silently chewing on his back teeth hard enough to look like he was chewing gum, which he wasn't. He looked like a hit man on the way to work.

I have never had a high tolerance for silence, so I said, "Well, that was really something, wasn't it?"

Mike pursed his lips together and squinted even more. "Richmond, you have had some really goofy ideas but this beats them all. If this was your idea of a joke, it wasn't a good one. I don't want anyone we know to know we were at that meeting tonight. What gave those people the right to put their hands all over us? It gave me the willies. Waaaa! Yuck!"

Mike wiggled his body as if to shake off cooties. Then he

went silent again. We turned left onto Colorado Boulevard and drove east toward Bob's Big Boy. Everything was such a familiar part of my growing up. Lake Avenue, Berry and Grassmuck Music Company where I had taken accordion lessons, the Academy Theater where I had gone maybe two hundred times.

We passed Pasadena City College from which most of the Rose Queens had been chosen, and then Dino's Italian Restaurant, my family's favorite. I always ordered the same thing there: a Coke, a small pizza with just cheese and tomato sauce, and a bowl of minestrone soup. They kept bringing little baskets of freshly baked Italian bread. Driving by made me miss my dad. It reminded me of all the good times we had spent there together.

When I thought about my dad, I remembered what the speaker had said—that someone in the audience needed the direction a father could give and that God would be like a father to anyone who would give his life to him. He said God could be our best friend too and would never let us down. With Mike and Eric so angry at me, I was feeling alone and especially in need of a father's wisdom and direction and encouragement. A dad's hug wouldn't have been too bad, or even a pat on the back.

I sighed and continued to watch the Pasadena business community whiz by as we headed for Bob's. Eric wasn't much for holding grudges and was always up for a good time. He blurted out, "Let's go jump on the trampoline." That was a big fad in Southern California in 1960 and for a dollar you could jump up and down for thirty minutes. Mike was tired of being a grouch and skidded to an abrupt halt in front of the thriving business. We paid our money and waited for three trampolines to open up.

The trampolines were at ground level, suspended over pits

six feet deep. Frankly, we were in no hurry to jump because three of the cutest girls at Pasadena High School were finishing their last ten minutes. I'd have paid a dollar or two just to watch them. I looked over at Mike and Eric. They looked like pointers that just found quail. I smiled because I knew Mike was going to be in a better mood for the rest of the night as long as I didn't bring up the church service again.

We were all disappointed when the buzzer sounded, telling us that it was our turn. A cute blonde jumping smiled at me and took three extra jumps, her ponytail bouncing playfully off of her back and then standing straight up. She fell to a heap, exhausted, and she and her three friends laughed at each other. As she ran passed me she said "tootles," and waved. I was in love, but it only lasted thirty seconds because these visions of beauty jumped in their '51 Chevy coupe and drove off forever.

Mike was smiling at me. "I fell in love and I didn't even get her name," I said as I began some warm-up jumps.

Mike laughed a belly laugh. "Three boss chicks, huh?"

Mike pretty much just jumped, but Eric and I were divers and had developed a little routine which included back flips and front flips, all mixed in with twists and flops. We were usually the stars of the midway, so to speak. We worked up a pretty good sweat in thirty minutes. Then the stupid buzzer sounded, ending our turn.

We got back in the Packard and I sat on top of the back seat. When we drove into Bob's Big Boy drive-in, I waved to everyone like I was the Rose Queen of Pasadena. Mike thought it was funny, but he was a little shy and not really given to exhibitionism. Eric just doubled over with laughter as I threw kisses to the people in the other cars and called out, "I love you, my children." When we pulled into the space, I slid down into the seat and got ready for our car hop to come and take our order.

Why is it that all car hops chew big wads of pink gum? She smiled and said, "You guys know what you want?"

I blurted out, "Yes, but it's not on the menu." She blew a bubble and popped it at me. Mike asked her to excuse me and explained that this was my first day out of the asylum and I still didn't know what normal was. I went along with Mike and stared at her as if I was crazy and might attack at any moment. Eric cracked up.

We always ordered the same things, never wavered, never varied. We could have ordered in unison, "A Big Boy with cheese, french fries, and a chocolate shake, please." The food was all good, but their shakes were the best—so thick you couldn't suck them through a straw no matter how hard you tried. They were more like soft serve ice cream than malts and rose an inch or two above the top of the stainless steel goblet in which they were served.

Our food was served on a tray mounted on the window. We were in heaven. It was a primal experience. We didn't talk, we moaned, we oooed, we closed our eyes and savored each bite. We didn't have any girls to impress so we filled our mouths much too full so that every taste bud was in contact with either a Big Boy hamburger or french fries.

The feeding frenzy was always over too soon, and sometimes if we had extra money we duplicated the experience. Not much about youth attracts me to relive it. But if I could eat like I did then and not blow up like a balloon, I would return to that one part. We left Bob's Big Boy happy and thankful Bob Wyan had come to earth and played around in his kitchen. It was good to be alive.

We drove to the Rose Bowl to see if anybody was racing. We parked under an oak tree near the end of the quarter-mile mark and waited for some action. We were not disappointed. Dennis Swensen was out and about in his heavily customized, fuel-injected '57 Chevy. Dennis had the car to beat and it was beautiful. It had several coats of black lacquer paint and Dennis never allowed a speck of dust to rest anywhere on his clean machine. He had beaten everyone in Pasadena, and guys came from surrounding cities to challenge him. This night a challenger from Glendale came in a '32 Ford duece coupe powered by a Buick engine with three two-barrel carburetors. It was yellow and covered with chrome.

"I think Dennis is in for it tonight," I said as they drove by to check for the police.

Mike was a fan of Dennis' and said, "He races for bucks. He's checked out this guy even though he is from out of town. If he thought he'd lose, Dennis wouldn't be here." Mike knew a little of his methods so I just nodded as we watched them u-turn and roll into position to race. We saw the silhouette of Dennis' friend standing about ten feet in front of both cars. We heard the finely tuned engines revving up. We saw the silhouette raise his arms, and our hearts began to pump as the arms went down.

Both sets of headlights raised up and engines roared to life and headed at us with a fury. We heard the screech of rubber when they began and each time they shifted. In about thirteen seconds two cars went by us both traveling more than a hundred miles an hour. Dennis Swensen was about a half a car length ahead, his legend secure until next week. We cheered because he was one of ours, a student who went to John Muir High School and we knew him. His '57 was the hottest car in Pasadena until the accident.

We left the Rose Bowl that night feeling good. The church experience seemed a distant memory. It had been a good night. Mike dropped me off at my house at about one in the morning. I was tired.

JUST ME AND GOD

I slipped in the house quietly, hoping not to disturb my brother, who took more of an interest in my comings and goings than I liked. I heard him snoring and relaxed. Then I slipped beneath the covers and snuggled into a comfortable position. No sooner had I closed my eyes than my mind returned to the speaker's promise that God wanted to be my father and to give me guidance and a purpose. I remembered that God wanted to forgive my sins, and thought that might keep him busy for some time.

I tried to shake off the religious thoughts but they wouldn't go away. I had the most urgent feeling that I had to stop trying to go to sleep and go ahead and do what the speaker said to do. My heart was telling me to ask Jesus into my life and ask him to forgive my sins.

I wasn't religious, but I knew that when you talked to God you ought to be on your knees. At 1:30 a.m. I got out of bed and onto my knees. It was pitch dark. The only sound in the room was the ticking of an alarm clock and my own rapid heartbeat. It was hard to know where to start. I felt I had to be honest and respectful to God.

"God, I hope you're out there somewhere. I think you are. If that guy was giving the straight scoop tonight, you want me to ask forgiveness of my sins and ask you to come in and take my life and clean it up. I don't know why you would want me. I'm not that good a kid, but the guy tonight said you've taken worse. I can't even remember all the sins I've committed. There's been a lot of them. Could you forgive them and then take my life and be my father and my friend? I'm not sure who I'm supposed to invite in because the guy tonight mentioned God, Jesus, and the Holy Ghost, but you know who's supposed to come in and anything is fine with me. Please come into my life. Amen."

I wasn't sure what to expect—harp music, chimes, a deep voice, maybe trumpets, but none of that kind of thing happened. It just stayed dark and quiet except for the clock on my night stand, which kept on ticking, marking the passing of time. But I felt different in a special way. Everything was going to be better now. I knew it way down deep and I didn't feel the least bit alone. If I was forced to choose one word to describe how I felt at 1:30 a.m. that grand night, it would be "safe." I had made the right decision and I knew it.

Thirty years have passed, and I have never been sorry for giving up the rights to my life to God. In no way has he ever disappointed me, nor has he ever given me a reason to be ashamed of him. God has remained faithful to me, even though there are countless times I have shamed him and given him reason to be embarrassed. It was a great night. I'll never forget it.

17

The Forest Fire

I T WAS DEEP AUGUST and the California sun had baked nearly every ounce of water out of the southern slopes of the San Gabriels. The mountains were ripe for a fire.

A group of misguided youth who had run out of constructive ways to spend their summer vacation decided to do something destructive and senseless. They spread gasoline on some dry brush and struck just one tiny match. It exploded into a raging inferno that raced through canyons and over hillsides—like a stallion gone mad, trying to see how far it could go before it was brought to bay.

Four of us were playing Monopoly at Mike Meagher's house, the most American of pastimes next to baseball. It teaches you greed and fills you with pleasure at the thought of seeing all your closest friends go bankrupt while you grow fat on their incompetence and bad luck. The game also wastes a pile of time as you wait for school to start again, something you actually begin to look forward to after having run out of ideas for meaningful recreation.

I smelled smoke, so we all jumped up and ran outside to see if we could locate the source. It wasn't difficult. Two miles northeast of us in the foothills of the San Gabriels, an impressive column of smoke was even beginning to block out the sunlight. The smell of burning brush was overwhelming.

No one spoke; truly kindred spirits don't have to. We just jumped on our bikes and peddled northeast for all we were worth. It wasn't every day you could see a forest fire, and this one looked like you could get a spectacular view. As we rode it was obvious that the fire was above Jet Propulsion Laboratories, where space and rocket research took place. The thought of it going up in smoke was inconceivable. It was a mysterious place, top secret, hush hush. Who could know what was stored there—atom bombs, rocket fuel for sure, and a whole stock pile of other explosives that were sure to take us with them if they ever blew.

Out of breath but full of enthusiasm, we were all brought to an abrupt stop by the Altadena Sheriff's Department. We were not the only ones wanting to see a real forest fire for ourselves. More than twenty kids about our age stood before the sheriff assigned to protect us. We were all begging for a chance to endanger our lives by getting a really good view, but it was clear he wasn't going to give in to the insane, suicidal club of lunatics that groveled before him. He actually got a little testy and told us to leave the area quickly or our parents would be notified.

We withdrew slowly, looking over our shoulders now and then to get the best glimpse we could of the raging inferno. More and more teams of fire fighters were arriving who would go hand to hand with the fire. The temperature was already in the nineties. One could only imagine what a miserable time the guys on the front lines would be having. Mike Meagher stopped walking and looked with longing at the raging fire. "I really wanted to get a good look at the fire. Too bad we didn't get here sooner before the sheriff's department. It will probably be out before tonight." Mike had that look. He could think up some pretty fun ideas.

"What are you thinking?" I probed.

"If the fire was still going tonight... it probably won't be. But if it was, it would be pretty easy to sneak past the sheriff guys. There is an empty lot up by Barbie Post's house. At the back of the empty lot is a trail which leads down into the canyon to the fire road. I'd sure like to see a fire up close, like close enough to feel the heat. You know what I mean?"

"What time were you thinking of doing this?" I inquired.

"After midnight. It's not like our parents are going to say, 'Hey why don't you and your friends go sneak past the police and check out a real forest fire. Get real close so you can feel the heat.'"

Ronny Dahn laughed and said, "That's not what my parents would say. If I asked they'd just ground me for the rest of my life and that would be the end of it. Nobody would ever hear from me again."

Doug Sigler just put cookies on the bottom shelf, an irresistible opportunity waiting to be grabbed. "This isn't the kind of thing you ask permission to do. You just do it and take your chances that you won't get caught. If they don't get the fire out, why don't we meet and go check out a forest fire up close?"

"Sounds good to me," I added, laughing because I couldn't believe we were even considering doing this. I think way down deep every one of us was hoping the fire would be out so we wouldn't really have to go through with this hairbrained adventure. We all knew it was crazy.

I have often wondered why our decision-making capacity didn't improve since our junior high years. I have a theory. Somewhere in your brain is a little chamber. Over the door it reads *GOOD DECISIONS INSIDE.* But it's locked tight and you don't get the key until you get older. That's why God gives you parents. Most, not all, of them have their keys and use those chambers all the time. None of us had the keys and seemed to have no access to our little chambers.

We agreed that we would listen to the news. If the fire wasn't going to be out, we would meet at 12:30 a.m. at the little league diamond above Lincoln and Altadena Drive. We would meet in the dug-out because no one could see you in there at night even when they drove by.

The fire was all they talked about on the news that night. It was entirely out of control, fanned by heavy winds. Tons of units were being brought in from as far as Arizona to help put it out. There was no doubt we had a date with adventure.

My mother was in Camarillo State Mental Hospital and my dad got up at 5:30 a.m. and went to bed early, about 9:30 p.m. My bedroom was at the front of the house and my window was ideal for crawling out. The hardest part was figuring out a way to stay awake until midnight. I decided on listening to the radio, but had to keep it quiet so as not to keep my brother awake. I listened to Wink Martindale on KRLA, Pasadena's leading rock station. Between Jerry Lee Lewis and the Del Vikings, I did pretty well. As midnight approached my adrenaline increased and it became easier to stay awake. At about ten till midnight, I slipped on jeans and a tee-shirt and turned off my radio. I gently pushed open the screen and slipped into the night.

The walk to the little league park was just less than a mile. The fire had spread and it seemed that the whole mountain had become involved. The midnight sky was alive with an eerie glow. It was quiet, unnaturally quiet—the occasional bark of a dog being the only sound. My own footsteps, breathing, and heartbeat provided the rhythm of the night.

I was the first one to get to the park, but that wasn't unusual. For some reason I was always the first one to get anywhere. I sat in the dug-out and watched an occasional car go up Lincoln Avenue. The smell of smoke was strong. The ballpark actually looked foggy because the smoke was so thick. My eyes were teary from the smoke and my nose began to run. My asthma started acting up.

Doug showed up next and asked, "Can you believe we're doing this?"

"I just hope we don't get caught. I don't think my dad would find this a really good place for me to be tonight." Doug lived with his mother and older sister. Even if he was caught his mom wouldn't be too hard on him. It wasn't her nature and she didn't have the energy to keep Doug completely under control. Doug never did anything malicious or terribly illegal, just nutty things that boys in the fifties did to have fun or get their kicks.

Ronny Dahn ran into the dug-out and sat down. He combed his hair just like the Fonz and that's what he did as soon as he sat down. He started combing his hair. I looked at him in amazement. "We're not going to be seeing any girls, Ronny. Why in the world are you combing your hair? By the time we get through crawling through the bushes we're going to look like we exploded, man!"

"You never know, Gare. Could be a bunch of the bossest chicks from La Canada Junior High are crawling across the Arroyo right now because they heard I'm out late tonight. Like you never know when you're going to see chicks."

"Brother!" I exclaimed. "I bet if your comb could talk it would say, 'Gimme a break.' Wonder where Mike is? This is his party."

Mike was ten minutes late, which made us mad because we were all nervous. We were kind of up for the adventure but we also wanted to get it over with so we could get to bed knowing we weren't going to be grounded for a year or two. When Mike got there we found out he had a hard time leaving home because his Shetland Sheepdog had barked a lot. He had waited for her to calm down so he could get away.

We split the dug-out and headed up Lincoln to Barbie Post's street. We were shocked to see a police car just to the other side of her house. We all hit the dirt and peered over a hedge to see what he was doing. He was smoking a cigarette. You could see the tip get brighter now and then and a puff of blue smoke come streaming out of the open window. He was looking down the street the other way.

"Let's go!" said Mike. "Stay quiet." We followed him past Barbie's house and walked in the dark shadows to the back of the empty lot. We could see the policeman hadn't moved an inch and had no idea we were there. We crawled along the back of the empty lot to the trail that led down to the canyon and disappeared into the night. Nobody knew we were gone or in the canyon.

The fire was about a mile away but the smoke was heavy and burned our throats as well as making our eyes teary. We slid down a trail we had been down a dozen times before in the daytime but never at night. The night changes things. Nothing seemed familiar and we had no idea how close to the bottom of the trail we were. It seemed to take forever.

"There rattlesnakes down here, Gary?" asked Ronny. I was the resident nature expert.

"Lots of them," I answered with authority and without hesitation.

"How do you know?" he followed suspiciously, like I might just be trying to scare him.

"I've seen them here before. And you want to know something else? They'll be crawling this way to get away from the fire. You should be okay if you don't step on one."

"What if you slide over one? We haven't been walking since we started down this trail."

"Sliding over one would be lots worse because he'd have time to bite you two or three times before you could get off of him."

Ronny sounded betrayed. "Nobody said anything about snakes when we planned this. Snakes aren't a part of the deal as far as I'm concerned."

Mike looked back at Ronny and calmly remarked, "What a wuss. I'm going down the trail first. If I get bit I'll let you know, okay? Until then shut up about snakes. Gives me the creeps."

We kept sliding down the trail convinced that sooner or later we would feel a rattler sinking its fangs into our hands or arms. Took some of the fun out of the adventure, to tell you the truth. I wished I hadn't said anything.

We finally reached the bottom, after about one hundred

yards of sliding and crawling. We were now on the fire road which would lead us to a trail that we could take to the top of a hill. There we would have a view of the raging forest fire that no one could possibly beat. We dusted ourselves off and began to walk up the fire road. The wind had changed and the smoke was blowing away from us. The moon gave us just enough light to see where we were going.

We suddenly heard a truck coming from behind us. Mike yelled, "Hide now!" We scattered in every direction. I dove into high grass and lay on my back with my heart pounding. The truck's headlights came around the bend, bouncing down the road as fast as it could. One of the fire fighters asked his buddy, "Hey, did you see a kid?" We didn't hear the answer and wondered if anybody would be sent back to look for us.

We came to the trail—steep, not at all well maintained, and hard to follow in the dark. Buck thorn, prickly pear cactus, spanish bayonet, and yucca plants scratched, poked, and speared us as we climbed the relentless hill. Our breathing grew labored as we pushed to our goal.

"Would this be a big snake area?" asked Ronny, still concerned about being bitten.

"Shut up about snakes, Ronny, or *I'll* bite you," said Mike. He was tired of Ronny bringing up snakes, probably because he was as afraid of them as Ronny was. We could hear the two sounds that combine to make the unmistakable noise of a forest fire: crackling and the rushing of wind.

By consuming oxygen at an unbelievable rate, fire creates its own wind. In fact, we sensed the wind at our back was on its way to feed the fire just ahead. Fire consumes everything—the trees, brush, animals, anything foolish enough to be in its ravenous, impersonal way. A forest fire doesn't have any feelings, but it does seem to have a mind of its own and an appetite for destruction second to none.

The hill up ahead was illumined by an intense glow, silhouetting Mike against the fiery sky. The roar was now so loud that we had to yell. When we reached the top, none of us were prepared for what we saw. The whole mountain in front of us was on fire, with flames ascending fifty feet in the air. We watched bushes explode when the fire touched them. And though the fire was two hundred yards away, we could feel the heat—hot enough to be uncomfortable and extremely oppressive.

The sight was spectacular, the most impressive thing any of us had ever seen in two ways. The sheer magnitude of that forest fire reminds me that I am small when I get to feeling big. It also serves as a monument to carelessness. Thousands and thousands of animals were losing their lives to the fire. Plants that had been there for more than two hundred years would never in my lifetime look healthy again.

We didn't speak but we felt powerful emotions: friendship, awe, sorrow, exhilaration. We also felt very powerless in the face of the most frightening predator that any of us had ever seen. That fire gave a new meaning to the word hell. It defined it. A fiery place of destruction that doesn't feel or care. Hell feeds on its victims, enjoys them, and takes their life and energy only to throw it away. We were watching an ultimate, unfeeling, impersonal selfishness unleashed by some unthinking boys who, for the sake of entertaining themselves, were willing to open Pandora's box on a wilderness that God had designed to bring glory to himself.

When we got there, I didn't feel like I thought I would. I was expecting to feel heroic, looking at the dragon, eye-to-eye. But it never looked at us. The impersonal fire took no notice whatsoever of our presence, didn't care we were there. It was moving away from us, killing a place of beauty I had visited scores of times before. I felt wilted in its evil presence.

"Well, we did it. We got the best view in town of a forest fire," said Mike sarcastically like it was a letdown. I could tell he felt the same way I did. "Time to go home, I expect."

Nobody protested. We didn't talk much on the way back.

The fire had put all of us in a glum mood. And yet something came out of that night that I will always be grateful for. The memory of friendships. What a gift of God.

None of us ever got caught. We just crawled back into our bedroom windows—dog dirty and exhausted, glad for having been together, but not really proud of what we had done. None of us would do it again. We all grew up.

18

Water Ballooning

UPON GRADUATION FROM HIGH SCHOOL, I was awarded a Youth for Christ leadership scholarship to Los Angeles Pacific College, a small Christian college that would someday merge with another to become Azusa Pacific University. The school was heavily infested with students who had been active in Youth for Christ during their high school years and a whole bunch of fun because of it.

My scholarship required that I run for student government, and I was elected the freshman class president. My office initiation included being dressed as a lady of the evening, after which I was hauled to U.C.L.A. and handcuffed with official L.A.P.D. handcuffs to the elevator of the girls' dorm. They all thought I was pledging an on-campus fraternity.

While handcuffed, with no way to release myself, a beautiful dorm proctor explained to me that it was illegal for me to be in the girls' dorm. They could call the campus police who would be more than delighted to enforce the law. Then I would forever be unable to enroll in the California State College System. I begged her forgiveness and told her that I would be more than glad to leave except for the handcuffs.

After more than two hours there, I was beginning to wonder if my initiators were taking into account a person's normal biological functions. I complained in jest to the dorm proctor about the lack of restroom facilities in elevators. She, being somewhat liberated, inquired as to the seriousness behind my complaint.

When I told her I was experiencing some mild anxiety about my plight, she asked me what I might do should my initiators be of the cruel variety. I told her that I expected to dance enthusiastically from foot to foot for as long as I could, then I would do whatever was necessary to protect the structural integrity of my bladder.

The young lady nodded sagely and began to view my plight in a more sympathetic light. She assured me that if push came to shove, she would protect my interests and guard my dignity and manly pride—which I took to mean she would bring me an empty container and keep the door of the elevator closed. She said she was a pre-med student, so I needn't be embarrassed to discuss such matters.

I told her it was too late, as I was already experiencing a medium state of embarrassment from which I expected to recover. I thanked her for her concern and continued to greet and say goodbye to an endless stream of the cutest coeds in the United States, none of whom could possibly be attracted to a freshman class president from a small Christian college dressed and made up to look like a hooker. Bummer!

I was rescued none too soon after my rain dance had begun in earnest. I was then taken to various other locations, including restaurants and department stores. After my friends felt I had experienced a sufficient dose of humiliation, I was finally allowed to return to civilian life as I had known it.

I was in charge of the initiation the next year. Since I had thought it not in good taste to dress a male as a lady of the evening, I decided to take a different tack. We rented a cave man outfit for the new freshman class president to wear and

drove him to San Diego. We took all of his money and identi-
fication and dropped him off downtown where the sailors
came to recreate. His required mission: to raise enough money
for bus and cab fare back to the college dorms in Los Angeles.

The guy's name was Doug Meadows, our school's answer
to Tom Cruise. Even dressed as Fred Flintstone, in less than
an hour he had raised thirty-five dollars, with the help of a
beautiful blonde waitress who fell instantly in love with him.
She treated him to dinner and even drove him to the bus station, kissing him on the cheek when he left. Being the consci-
entious type of initiators, we stayed just in case a rescue was
necessary, so we watched the whole disgusting display of
manipulation and usury.

I suggested we initiate Doug again since his initiation had
been too easy. I argued that there should be some humiliation involved, some discomfort, and was accused of being
jealous because his initiation was more fun than mine. It was
true that I was a little envious. It would have been nicer to be
befriended by a beautiful, blonde, kissy waitress than a liberated dorm proctor with a bed pan.

But I was still adamant that initiations should carry with
them a level of discomfort well beyond what Doug had experienced. I maintained that he might feel cheated and not feel
sufficiently initiated unless we did more. In the end I was
voted down four to one. We followed the bus he took from
the bus station and stayed to watch Doug hail a cab. We even
watched the cab take him back to campus. The good looking
people really have it easy. I'll never know.

FRED AND ART

I roomed in the dorms my first year in college and took
my meals in the college dining room. But to save money, the

second year I took an apartment with two good friends, Fred Wright and Art Harrell. Fred was the student body president and Art was vice president. Two nicer roommates could not be located this side of the milky way. They were also responsible to the point of being overly responsible. If left unchecked, this condition can become a severe personality disorder, leaving the person, what people call, a dull bore.

Art had plenty of potential for cure but Fred worried me. He was given to excessive devotional periods, with a lot of praying and reading his Bible. He was always on time, did what he said, never used questionable language, was moral, and always asked the question, "Will I get into any trouble if I do that?" As you can see, he was one game short of a double header and in jeopardy of growing up with no stories to tell his future children about how his life had changed for the better. Your kids don't want to hear stories involving regular devotions and total responsibility. It's too much to live up to, too much to ask them to believe.

Yes, my roommates needed me and I needed them. We balanced each other. I was backpacking the Grand Canyon of life on the edge. Responsibility was not my middle name, but I did know how to have fun. I think that's why these guys asked me to join them. There seemed to be no other plausible reason.

Before I tell you how I got Fred arrested, let me describe what life was like with these two guys. I would get back to the apartment from class carrying a stack of books, all of which had enough assigned reading to keep me busy into the night. I always thought I would get to it, but there were always friends to call, girls in the dorms to minister to, work, and the need for something, anything, to break the routine.

I was a master at breaking the routine. Fred and Art would be hard at work, books spread out everywhere and them staring at the books and writing furiously about whatever the books were saying. Art was really funny. He stacked his books in order, with the subjects that he liked the least at the top and the subjects he loved at the bottom. He said it helped him to have something to look forward to, saving the best for last. He would insert pages entitled lunch and dinner between the books where he thought a break would be appropriate.

This system worked well for Art. He was our school valedictorian and graduated magna cum laude. Laude was not in my future. In my case it was, "Laude, will he ever make it?" Fred and Art tried their best to help me, and they did. They rubbed off on me and I on them.

On Halloween night in 1964, I made a terrific breakthrough with Fred. And how he needed it! It was about nine-thirty at night and I was just getting back to the apartment after speaking to a group of high school students at a San Gabriel Youth for Christ Halloween party. They had brought a bunch of their friends who didn't know Christ and when I shared my faith in a fun way I was blessed by God. I left thankful for the privilege of being allowed to introduce these kids to Christ.

Back at college I was anxious to find out where the fun was so I could get into the middle of it. I ran into the apartment and discovered that Art was out having fun. But Fred, good ol' predictable Fred, was studying.

"Fred, what are you doing here? There are places to go, things to do, and fun to be had. You don't stay home on Halloween night, for goodness' sake."

Now Fred was the serious type for the most part and a lot of the time he tolerated me. "I'm not sure Christians should celebrate Halloween," he offered matter-of-factly. "It's a pagan holiday," he added.

"Pagan, smagan. It's a day for fun, nothing more, nothing less. I'm nineteen, Fred. I never worshiped any demons, or have I honored them in any way. All I have ever done is collected a bunch of candy and played a trick or two. Somehow I don't see Jesus getting frosted over kids dressing up and asking for candy. I don't see him dressed up like a witch, but I see him coming to the door and helping kids to have a good time. It's neighborly and joyful and Christ said that he came that our joy may be full. Listen, Fred, I'm going to tell it to you straight. You're predictable and boring and in serious danger of missing out on the fun side of life. Picture this. You're thirty-seven and your twelve-year-old son comes and says, 'Dad, tell me about your life. Come on Dad, what did you do for fun?' You're in trouble, Fred, and you know it."

Fred looked a little worried. Actually I think it was the "boring and predictable" line that got to him right off and I needn't have said much more. I went for the kill. "Fred, don't keep putting off till tomorrow what you know you should be doing today. You'll just end up with a bunch of empty yesterdays." I got that line from the *Music Man*. Professor Harold Hill said it to Marion, the librarian, on the footbridge when he was trying to get her to kiss him, and it worked.

Fred asked, "What do you want to do?"

"Go water ballooning, Fred. Come with me."

"Count me in."

Boy, would he be sorry. Or maybe not. You'd have to ask him. It's just that water ballooning didn't turn out the way that I had planned it in my mind. But it rarely does, does it?

When Fred asked what the plan was, I told him that when I was in high school at the Pasadena Academy of the Nazarene on the same campus as Pasadena Nazarene College, I had found the ultimate fun place to water balloon. He inquired

Where and I told him. The Nazarene kids can't do anything without breaking a rule. They can't go to shows. They can't dance. They are discouraged from bowling and pretty much everything else people do for fun. So in the final analysis they are left with necking.

"Necking?" queried Fred.

"Yes. They park on Brezee Avenue next to the school and neck."

"What's necking?"

"Kissing, smooching, hugging, staring into each other's eyes and saying romantic things. Fred, don't tell me you never…"

"Of course I have. I just didn't call it that. I didn't call it anything. I just did it."

"With who?"

"With whom?"

"Don't change the subject, Fred."

"That's a private question."

"It doesn't matter anyway. Here's the deal. You know how hot it is tonight? It's hot enough so that twenty cars will be parked on Brezee Avenue, all of them with at least one couple listening to romantic music and kissing each other till their lips get sore. That's all Nazarenes can do for fun. They're waiting for us like sitting ducks on a pond. All we need is about fifty water balloons, and the evening is ours."

There sat Fred, picturing passionate people plastered properly and picturesquely. No more Mr. Predictable for Fred. He looked at me through eyes reborn and said, "What are we waiting for? Let's go get the ammo."

When a person makes a breakthrough of this nature, it is not unusual for one to go overboard a little. Fred bought a hundred water balloons, which took about an hour to fill. A little past 10:30 p.m., we headed up the Pasadena freeway on our way to the lovers' lane massacre. Fred was lighthearted. What an instant transformation. We laughed all the way to Pasadena Nazarene anticipating the action. We were looking forward to screaming girls and yelling guys having their passions cooled by our missiles of mirth.

Fred finally turned left off of Washington Boulevard onto Brezee Avenue. We had two plastic waste baskets full of water balloons, one in the back seat and one in the front. We were ready.

"Fred, go about seven to ten miles per hour. Any faster and I'll never be able to put the balloons through the windows."

"Right," he said, like we were going to be bombing Russia or something.

"Also Fred, get as close to the cars as you can. It makes it easier and we can hear the screaming and yelling better," I further instructed.

"Right," he said with willing deadly abandon.

There were more cars with necking couples than I had ever seen before—maybe twenty-five or so. When we passed the first one I hurled in a water balloon which burst on the edge of the open window and showered the couple. She screamed and he yelled just as we had anticipated.

Fred was in heaven, laughing as I hurled balloons in rapid succession. I rarely missed my mark as we achieved our objective car by car. Fred was loving it.

When we finally passed all the cars, we still had seventy-five water balloons left. "Now what do we do?" asked Fred.

"We go park for ten minutes and let them get back to necking. Then we hit them again."

"So soon?"

"Yeah. They never expect you'll do it again. And it's too warm to roll up the windows. Mark my words. They'll be sitting ducks ten minutes from now."

We parked and waited ten minutes. Then I insisted Fred
let me drive so he could throw the balloons. That was the
really fun part because you could watch what was happening.
We changed places and took off for a second pass.

Fred was great. He had a natural talent for hurling balloons and created more havoc than I did. Fred was in ecstasy.
We laughed until we could hardly breathe, and then laughed
some more.

We still had fifty balloons left.

"Do we go back again, Gary? We have all these balloons
left."

"No, Fred, it would be one too many passes. We should go
back to the dorms at our school. We could get a little action
going there."

"How would it look for the student body president to be
throwing water balloons?"

"It would improve your image. You will appear more balanced. People need to see your fun side. They've seen your
serious side for four years now. Take my word for it, Fred. It
will be okay."

Fred resigned himself to loosening up a little. We changed
places and he drove again. I think he thought I drove a little
fast. He drove a European car called a Borgward and he was
a little picky about it. It was a nice car.

As we drove by the California Institute of Technology,
someone hurled an egg at Fred's car. It hit the windshield
and the slimy yoke splattered everywhere. Fred wheeled
around to see if we could locate the egger. All we saw was a
black Volkswagen pulling out of a driveway near where we
had been hit. Two guys about our age were in the front seat
and we were sure that they had been the offenders. Now we
had an excuse to use one of the fifty water balloons we had
left.

The Volkswagen accelerated in our direction on the other side of the street and Fred accelerated as well. We were both doing about fifty. When Fred laid out a water balloon, the impact on the antennae and the windshield was like being hit by a balloon traveling one hundred miles an hour. It made an incredible noise and caused the oncoming driver to momentarily lose control. He swerved back and forth, then skidded to a stop, but only for a second. Then he made an unbelievable u-turn and began to chase us.

Fred made a sound—"Waaaaaa," as I remember—and punched it, as we say in the racing world. We were not going to be caught by anybody that seemed that intent on catching us. Before we could begin to out-accelerate the black VW, it got within thirty yards of us.

As we passed under a street light I recognized the driver. It was Dennis Delyay. I had met him in summer school and played against him in every sport. He had a very bad temper. His favorite pastime was street fights and I had no memory of his ever having lost one. When I told Fred this he made another sound and pressed the pedal to the metal.

We were pulling away from Delyay's Bug but he gained on us every time we were forced to turn. In a panic Fred turned into a gas station to cut a corner—only to find out there was no driveway out the other side. He skidded to a stop as Delyay skidded in behind us. He leapt from his car with the athletic grace of a leopard. I saw that he had grown. He was over six feet now and built for body contact sports.

Fred made another sound—"Yaaaaa," as I recall—which I took as a primal emotional escalation two letters removed from "Waaaaa." Fred threw his car in first gear, burned rubber, and exited the gas station off of what seemed like the highest curb in Pasadena. We bottomed out and sparks flew in every direction.

Dennis followed in the same manner, indicating he was out for blood and guts. Letting him catch us was not a consideration. I wondered where Fred had acquired such good driving skills. He wasn't so predictable after all.

He turned to me and said, "If we can just get to the Pasadena freeway we can lose this guy. I get him on the top end but he catches me on the curves."

"Fred, we *have* to lose this guy. He's bad news. He's always been bad news. He likes busting heads. It's his favorite pastime."

Fred looked determined, as determined as anyone has ever looked. He also had that I'm-too-young-to-die look and sped across Green Street faster than anyone ever had before him. That dead-ended into Arroyo Avenue just up ahead and the light turned green at the perfect moment. But at the intersection was a police car, so Fred slowed down for the left turn. We drove sanely through the intersection.

Then the unbelievable happened. Dennis Delyay's buddy was hanging out of their car waving his hands at the police car and motioning toward us. The police caught on real quick and pulled us over.

There were two policeman in the black and white and one stayed by us as we sat inside the Borgward. Fred watched his rearview mirror and described to me how the policeman was removing an orange piece of water balloon from the antennae of Dennis Delyay's Volkswagen. Fred told me that Dennis looked real angry and was giving the officer an earful. When Delyay was finished with his story, the policeman came over and asked us to get out of Fred's car. He looked inside the car and of course the first thing he found was a large rubber waste basket with forty-nine water balloons in it.

"These yours?" the officer asked.

We nodded, although a dozen sarcastic answers came to

mind, all of which I decided to keep to myself. Fred was glad.

The officer handed the balloons to his partner who put them in their trunk. He told us to stand by the Borgward while he went back and got a clipboard and his ticket book. He made each of us tell what happened, but he took the reports one at a time so that we couldn't hear each other's story.

When he was done, the policeman wrote us both citations for throwing a substance at a moving vehicle and made sure that we knew we would be appearing in court to face the charges. If convicted, we would both have a police record since throwing a substance at a moving vehicle was considered a misdemeanor.

Fred was not good at getting into trouble. He became icy silent and would not speak to me for two days. I kept telling him that he would have a great story to tell his kids someday, but this did not comfort him. Nor did it assuage his slow-burning anger.

Our roommate Art thought it was the funniest thing in the world, and Fred didn't appreciate that either. He was even cold to Art, who kept kidding him about having a police record. The continuation of our fellowship was in question. Fred saw himself as seduced into a temporary lapse of sin, with me as the agent of his temptation. I guess that's the way it was. But having been raised to take responsibility for my own choices, I didn't like getting blamed for the whole thing.

I finally spoke up. "Fred, for goodness' sake. Don't be so distant. You're two years my senior. You could have said no. Everybody just takes their lumps. Whatever will be will be. I thought it was a fun night and you were having a pretty good time until we got busted. We'll get past this."

Fred lightened up and the tension abated. I enjoyed the fact that he even began to tell a few close friends about our

Halloween adventure and caught myself smiling at him whenever he did.

THE JUDGE

When our day in court arrived, we drove in different cars—which was good because of the way things turned out. We drew the toughest judge in the history of Pasadena's municipal court system. Judge Joseph A. Sprankle, Jr., enjoyed his tough-on-crime image. He knew little of mercy and nothing of grace.

I had been in his court before as a witness but not a criminal. I had witnessed an assault and battery against my next-door neighbor by a man who had been tried unsuccessfully for the crime of murder. Judge Sprankle had thought him guilty of the former charge and said so in court right after the jury had acquitted him. But Sprankle nailed him on the assault and battery charge and gave him a stiff penalty. As soon as I saw the judge, I didn't have the feeling that our day in court was going to go well. It didn't.

First of all our case was called very late. Although we were required to be at the courtroom by 2:00 p.m., we weren't called until 5:00. The judge looked and sounded like he needed dinner. He was grouchy with everyone, including his own staff. Nobody was winning their case or even getting a break. Fred sat next to me, as quiet as a church mouse and nervous as a long-tailed cat in a room full of rocking chairs. He was simply not good at being in trouble, having very little experience at it. I should have been more understanding. He looked so guilty you'd have thought he'd killed somebody or knocked off a bank.

All of a sudden the bailiff called out those frightening words, "The State of California versus Gary Richmond." I wanted to call out, "How do you like those odds!" But I decided against it, considering Judge Sprankle's state of humor.

Judge Sprankle cleaned his silver no-rimmmed glasses and read the details of our case. Then he took off his glasses and turned to me. "Mr. Richmond, it says here that you are charged with throwing a substance at a moving vehicle. How do you plead?"

"Well, your honor, first I would like to have the word substance changed to water balloon. Substance sounds like a rock or a can of gasoline. It was a water balloon on Halloween night. It was more of a childish prank than an act of violence you see, and when people look at this case in the future it just seems to me it would be more accurate if it read 'water balloon.'"

"Mr. Richmond, I get the feeling that you aren't taking this very seriously. Your throwing of a water balloon could have caused a serious accident leading to the loss of life. It says in the report that Mr. Delyay temporarily lost control of his vehicle after being struck by your missile."

"Water balloon, your honor. That's because Mr. Delyay wanted to catch us. He was so angry he threw on his brakes so he could come after us. To be perfectly honest, your honor, if the record reads that I threw the water balloon it reads inaccurately. I didn't throw it."

The Judge leaned back in his huge leather chair and said, "Then you're saying your friend Mr. Wright threw the water balloon?"

All of a sudden I felt like a fink. There was no way I was going to accuse Fred. "Your honor, I merely said that *I* didn't throw it. I cannot admit to something I didn't do." I still felt finky so I added, "It wasn't my turn. Had it been my turn, I must be honest and tell you that I would have thrown it."

The courtroom filled with laughter and even old iron jaw smiled for a fleeting moment. Judge Sprankle locked all of his fingers in a praying position and sat quietly. Then he spoke. "Mr. Richmond, what do you think I should do to you?"

"Your honor, as you must already know, I have never been in trouble with the law. We thought Dennis Delyay and his friend had egged us, and we were just acting like kids by retaliating—something we'll think twice about again, I assure you. If I were you, I'd warn us real good. I promise you, you'll never see us in here again."

"Oh, Mr. Richmond, how naive of you. If I let you off, you'll go tell all your college friends there's a pushover judge that sits behind a bench in the municipal courts of Pasadena. Then they'll declare open season on our little town and water balloons will be flying everywhere, wouldn't they?"

"Begging your honor's pardon, but this little legal thing just isn't the kind of thing I'm proud to talk about at our Christian college. No matter what you do, I'm not going to tell anybody anything about it. Then again, if you would permit me to say so, what would stop me from telling everybody you let me off?" The courtroom laughed again but Judge Sprankle didn't smile.

"You're too honest, Mr. Richmond. You wouldn't do that. Guilty as charged. Pay the bailiff fifty-five dollars. Next case, please."

I was in shock. In 1964, fifty-five dollars was a tidy sum of money. I had only fifty-seven dollars to my name, fifty of which was saved to make the very last payment on an engagement ring for my fiancée. Carol would be crushed to have to wait several extra weeks for me to save another fifty dollars.

I stayed to see how Fred's part went, but I can't remember much about it because I was so shaken up over the engagement ring. I just remember that Fred had to pay fifty-five dollars and he decided not to talk to me.

Of course I was finally forgiven. Even though lots of years pass between our visits, it is this incident and the time I bought the bobcat that bond us together. And if it weren't for me, he has told me he would have precious few of these kinds of stories, the ones his kids really like to hear.

Fred Wright is now a godly pastor in the state of Colorado, a steady father, and a fine husband. He has known difficult times since those carefree college days and has weathered them well. Lord knows I didn't corrupt him, but perhaps prepared him for the nutty kinds of people with whom pastors have to deal.

Fred and Art left their marks on me, good marks. They were both consistent, steady, faithful men, full of integrity and love for God. And needless to say, I marked them up a little too. I think they call my marks graffiti.

19

The Bobcat

SINCE EARLY CHILDHOOD, I have suffered under the illusion that if I could obtain a certain possession or experience, I would be fulfilled, completed, happy. I am now forty-seven. You would think I would have wisened and grown beyond these periodic wanderings into fantasyland. But I have not.

The smell of a new car, the shiny cover of a new book, the high-resolution picture screen on a television, the sleek lines of a new camera—all these things call to me like sirens of old called to sailors to steer their sailing ships into certain oblivion. For me, fighting these urges might compare to a reformed smoker's desire to light one up or a recovered alcoholic's desire to feel the warmth of whiskey as it sears the throat and settles into the system.

My *needs* have always been met, but never my *wants*. My wants seem endless. You would know that if you had ever watched me come alive leafing through a Sears catalog—one of my favorite pastimes.

I have had some strange wants fulfilled and am grieved to report that I was never ever made happy by them. In fact, they are now an embarrassment to me. Let me tell you the worst-case scenario. It happened twenty-eight years ago and still has a humbling effect whenever I recall it.

As a sophomore at Los Angeles Pacific College, I was living in a small one-bedroom apartment with two very stable and godly young men who were both seniors at the same Christian college. I was engaged to Carol, my bride of twenty-seven years now. Those who knew me then thought of me as a responsible, thoughtful, and dedicated young man. However, those who knew me *well* knew I was capable of some unusual behavior.

It was during that period that I decided that the purchase of a bobcat would make me happy. It did not.

For weeks, I combed the classified section of the *Los Angeles Times* under the heading "Exotic Pets," hoping to see bobcat kittens for sale. One Friday afternoon I did find an ad, and my heart leaped for joy within me. My fingers trembled with anticipation as I dialed the phone number that was listed.

A woman answered and confirmed all my imaginings— that bobcats were indeed the new wave of the pet trade. She adored her female, and I could hardly take down directions to their home fast enough because she had only two kittens left.

I rushed down as fast as I could to find that the young kittens had been sold. But the couple again lifted my spirits by telling me they had a teenaged bobcat on their back porch, which they would be willing to part with at a bargain price. Under the spell of having an unusual pet, I did not notice that their house smelled like a giant, unchanged, kitty litter box.

As I held their pet, a very affectionate adult female, I was certain beyond any doubt that a bobcat is what I wanted— i.e., had to have! They took me to the back porch and there in a small carrying cage was a nearly grown female. When she saw me, she snarled and hissed. Her ears went down and she glared and growled the whole time we were there talking.

The man assured me, "She'll tame down fine (LIAR!). She just doesn't like being in a small cage like that." Did I mention that the man looked like he could be Anton LeVey's brother?

This wasn't what I had driven forty miles to buy, but she would tame down. Well, the bobcat looked healthy—more like possessed. I paid $125 and left thinking what fun it would be to own a tame wildcat. I named her Tara. It seemed exotic and wild and fit perfectly.

When I finally got to our apartment, I was sad neither of my roommates was there to enjoy the surprise. I let the cat out of the carrying cage. She ran wildly around the room, searching for a place to escape. She opted to jump from the floor to the kitchen sink, then to a room divider just over the stove, about six feet above the ground. From there, she glared and continued to growl.

She would tame down, he had said (WRONG!). I offered the bobcat assorted parts of an uncooked chicken, but she only batted them away with a haughty, who-needs-it attitude. Well, give her time. Bummer!

I had to leave the apartment to run an errand. That's when my roommate Fred came home, unaware that the apartment was occupied. He innocently walked to the kitchen sink to pour a glass of water. That's when he heard the low, rumbling growl behind him. He turned around slowly and found himself face-to-face with the she-devil bobcat I had purchased for just $125.

Fred backed slowly out of the kitchen, staying as close to the wall and as far away as he could from the evil presence which had claimed our apartment. Beads of perspiration formed all over his face as he let himself out the front door. Art would never get a bobcat, so Fred knew that I would be able to unravel the mystery. He waited for me to get home—safe on our porch.

I returned from my errand excited to see Fred sitting on the front porch of our apartment. Something was obviously bothering him, so I asked him what was wrong. He looked at me as if I should know.

"Gary," he began in an exasperated way, "What's in our apartment? I went in to get something to drink and eat and began to hear a low, rumbling growl. I looked behind me, and ready to attack was some sort of wild animal. Is that a bobcat in there?"

"Yes, Fred, and she'll tame down soon. The family I bought her from said she's uptight from being in a small carrying cage. I got a great deal on her. She cost only $125."

"Gary, don't you think it would have been good to ask Art and me before getting a bobcat? Personally, I liked our apartment better when I felt safe in it. I don't think it's going to tame down. Don't they call bobcats *wildcats*?"

"Come on, Fred. Tara will tame down, and you'll love her. Fred, you are so responsible and predictable, you need a little excitement in your life. You'll be able to tell your grandchildren you lived with a bobcat during your college days. Give it a try. Really, what can it hurt?"

We kept eye contact and Fred, a little stung with the idea that he was too responsible and predictable, finally spoke. "Okay, we'll give it a try. If it doesn't work out, you and Tara will have to make other arrangements."

When we stepped into our small apartment, we were greeted by a significant odor. It was a good news, bad news thing. The good news was that Tara had used her kitty litter tray. The bad news was that she needed a tray six times larger and deeper to achieve sanitation. Kitty litter and odor were everywhere. I'm an optimist, but even I knew that this was not a good beginning. Fred didn't say anything but gave me a very skeptical look.

When Art got home he got a big laugh out of the whole deal and was more willing than Fred to give it a try. He laughed every time it growled at one of us, which it continued to do every day it lived with us, which was a little over a week.

Tara never allowed me to pet her or even touch her. Every effort ended with her taking a fearsome swipe at me, and then she would run and hide behind or under something. Most of the time, though, she just stared down from her favorite haunt—the room divider above the kitchen. Fred and Art locked themselves in the bedroom at night and left me on the couch with Tara lurking somewhere in the darkness. Our apartment smelled like a giant kitty litter box, and it was filled with tension.

Even an optimist usually knows when something isn't working. I knew the guys were anxious for me to admit that living in small quarters with a wild animal was not good. They wanted me to say, "Guys, you were right; this was a stupid thing to do." But I hate to admit it when I'm wrong, so it took a final straw.

Tara somehow got into the bathroom early in the morning when everybody else in the apartment needed to get ready for classes. She claimed it for her own and would not let any of us in for whatever reason. She was getting wilder and meaner each day. Even I was not sure whether or not she would attack. At any rate, all three of us left for class unwashed, unshaven, and undeodorized.

As he left, Fred spoke the words I knew were coming: "She has to go!"

When Art nodded, I shared something really difficult and painful for me to say. "You guys are right. I never should have bought her."

I called the man who sold me Tara; he was sad she wasn't working out. He said he knew a man who wanted her and would send him right over. Man, everything was going to work out fine, I thought. The man showed up and with a little effort—about an hour of terrifying running around—we finally got Tara back into her carrier. I told the man I'd sell her for only $125. He said that was more than a fair price, but he didn't have the money right then and would send it to me.

I didn't have much of a bargaining position, so I let him take the bobcat, which I didn't want any longer anyway. A week passed, but no money came. I called the telephone number he had given me. Guess what? Disconnected. I drove to the address he had given to me; he had been evicted.

My only satisfaction was that he had the bobcat.

And that's the only satisfaction that this story brings me because it highlights one of my greatest weaknesses, one I continue to fight: the subconscious conviction that a certain purchase will make me happy. I was nineteen when all of this occurred. I am now twenty-nine years older, and still at times I must fight to keep from being foolish and attempting to fill voids that are not there.

I am wiser now and know one thing for sure. If I live to be one hundred, I will never buy another bobcat.

20

Somebody up There Likes Me

I DON'T KNOW ABOUT YOU, but I shy away from people who tell hard-to-believe stories—the kind that defy reason, drift beyond coincidence, and stretch credibility. This book has been filled with them. I even find myself amazed that they are true.

But all these crazy stories convince me of one very important truth. They tell me that Somebody up there likes me and is very intent on seeing that both my needs and appropriate wants are met. That Somebody is the Lord Jesus. The Lord is my Shepherd, and I shall not want. God continues to watch over me and care for me. He may be slow, but he's never late.

Let me illustrate this principle by telling you how I got into the zoo. Full time ministry with Youth for Christ was fulfilling but a disaster to marriage. Working seventy to eighty hours a week left me little time at home with Carol and my beautiful baby girl, Marci. By the time we were four months behind in salary, facing the landlord became increasingly painful. I opted to be able to pay my bills and resigned.

I took the first job I could get: cleaning swimming pools. It was great to be home nearly every night, but I was very lonely. This new line of work offered no contact with people, except the occasional moment someone would pull back their curtain to see if I was doing my job.

After nearly a year I discussed my loneliness with Carol. I felt guilty for complaining because we were now paying the bills and seeing a lot more of each other than ever before. She listened empathetically and asked, "If you could do anything you would like to do, what would it be?"

"I'd really like to work with animals, like at a zoo."

"I heard this morning on television that they were opening a new zoo to replace the old Griffith Park Zoo. They interviewed the director. Maybe they're hiring. Do you want me to check on it?"

"Sure! That would be great."

Carol called the director of the zoo, Dr. Young, a charming old circus vet on the verge of retirement. The zoo belonged to the city of Los Angeles. Once signed up, I had to wait to take a civil service test in downtown Hollywood on a Saturday morning. I drove in a little early to give myself time to get lost and found again.

I was really excited with mixed emotions. I didn't know what to expect but didn't have anything to lose either. I parked my Volkswagen Bug and began to look for the line to take the animal keeper's exam. There were poorly marked lines everywhere, so you had to ask everybody what line they were in until you found the right one. One particular line went out of sight around the block. I wondered which line that could be—surely not the animal keeper's, a position that didn't pay much.

I was wrong. That was the line, already crowded with more than three hundred men and a handful of women. I took my place at the end, and being the friendly sort, began to make conversation with the man in front of me. Big mistake. "Hi, I'm Gary Richmond. This is the line for the animal keeper exam, isn't it?"

This guy was wearing a suit and tie and I was dressed very casually. He appeared to be in his late twenties, with thin rimmed glasses that make you look like you probably own a slide rule that you actually use. "Yes, this is the line," he answered with a drop or two of sarcasm.

"Do you know how many jobs are available at the new zoo?" I asked.

"Just two openings," he relayed.

I again looked at the line which had continued to grow quickly even since I had entered it. Over five hundred applicants for two job openings. I felt a little ill and thought to myself, I wonder if I ought to go home and make the best of what was really a beautiful day? But instead I continued the conversation with the man in front of me.

"So what do you do?" I probed.

"I just finished my masters degree in zoology at U.C.L.A. I've been a student for a long time and I'm looking for a little practical experience to go with the years of study I'm glad to have behind me. After the zoo I want to do research in the wild."

My eyes narrowed as I studied him. He had a very dignified name like Harlan Hampton the Third and I knew without asking that he was an A student at the top of his class. I just resigned myself to the fact that there were five hundred applicants for *one* job opening. I could see he was indulging me and wishing an intelligent person had stood behind him. I decided to pursue the man behind me.

"Hi, I'm Gary Richmond. Couldn't have asked for a better day for the test, could we?"

"No, we couldn't. My name's Tom Hanaford. I'm a high school biology teacher. I'm a little tired of the classroom and would like to get a little practical experience before I go back for my master's degree program. I'm hoping about half the questions on the test are questions I've asked my students over the last twelve years. I should be ready. I've read enough books on the subject, so many I wouldn't know what to read next. Say, what do you do, Gary?"

"I clean swimming pools. I was in high school youth work before that. Animals and nature have just been a hobby, sort of..." I felt like the ninety-eight pound weakling in the old Charles Atlas weight-lifting ad, right after the bully had kicked sand in his face.

This guy turned out to be more talkative than I was and went on and on about books he had read getting ready for the test, using Greek and Latin terms I had never heard of before. My only hope was that one of these guys would get run over by a Mack truck before they were hired for the two openings.

Then a horrible thought occurred to me. What if these two guys were the two dumbest guys in the line of over five hundred applicants? Considering the law of averages, these two were probably somewhere in the middle of the curve. I decided to make the most of that day just gaining a little test-taking experience and maybe apply for one of the shorter lines next time.

We were ushered into classrooms and given the test. I was surprised to discover that less than half the questions were about animals, and a good number of the animal questions were relatively easy, common sense ones. I didn't feel so stupid when I handed in my test and drove home. I would have to wait a month to see my placement on the written portion. If I made the cut, the oral exam should be easier.

Finally the notice arrived. I had passed, number forty-two out of five hundred and forty. It didn't look promising but it wasn't the humiliation I had expected either. They only interviewed three people per position, so I was a long way from even getting a chance to be heard, much less hired.

The day of the oral exam, I showed up in my Sunday best.

Everyone in the room appeared to be more qualified, and I felt pretty nervous. But then I thought to myself that I had nothing to lose and everything to gain. Maybe I could place high enough to be interviewed in the future. I had discovered that they would be adding keepers as the zoo enlarged and that my list would remain active for two years.

Finally my name was called late that afternoon. Each applicant had been given about fifteen minutes to prove that he had what it would take to care for rare and valuable animals. All three of the interviewers were older, and I figured they had been interviewing all day. I tried to think if that was good or bad. On the one hand they may be tired; on the other, if I were very impressive I would stand out. I really wanted this job. More lonely than ever as a pool man, I almost salivated over the rare chance to become an animal keeper at the Los Angeles Zoo.

After the introductions were completed, the questions began. "Son, why do you want to be an animal keeper?"

I had anticipated that question. "I hoped you would ask that question. Since I was a little boy I have loved animals. Even now if you went to the Altadena Public Library, you would find that I checked out and read every book they had on animals. Taking care of them has been a dream from childhood. Now more than ever, caring for animals would be a privilege because we are losing them all over the earth so quickly. If I don't get the chance now I fear there will be no chance in the future. Some men dream of being doctors, others firemen or policemen. But those things seem like nothing compared to the privilege of caring for rare and endangered animals. It would be the fulfillment of a life-long dream."

The men all wrote a note on my interview sheet and then asked me a second question. "What do you think animal keepers do?"

I had visited the zoo and asked, so I had some idea. "I

think they begin their day checking their animals to see that they are healthy. If they are not I suppose they see that the zoo's veterinarian is called or someone in authority is notified. If everything is normal I would think they would clean the fronts of the exhibits so that the animals might be nicely displayed by the time the zoo opens at ten o'clock in the morning. Then they would clean the night quarters and prepare their food for when they were let in. I would suspect many of the animals would be fed something during the day. I think animal keepers would spend some time checking their animals periodically to protect them from potential harm from the public. They would probably be expected to take note of important behaviors such as mating or fighting or anything out of the ordinary and check the security of the cages to guard against escape."

"Son, I didn't hear you say you should play with the animals sometime?"

"No, sir. I believe that it's the zoo's policy not to make pets of your animals for breeding considerations and safety. I suppose it poses a terrible temptation for some of the new keepers, but it would be a temptation I think I could resist in the best interest of the animals."

The men looked impressed with my answer and took more notes. "You know, son, most days you'll go home smelling real bad from animal excretions. How's your wife gonna like that?"

"She'll love it, and you know why? She knows how bad I want this job and she wants me to be happy. She's a great wife and is prepared to be a part of any sacrifice that the job may represent. I'm a lucky guy, gentlemen."

You could tell they liked that answer too. I didn't like the next question. "Mr. Richmond, you have a police record. Throwing a substance at a moving vehicle. Could you tell us a little about that incident?"

"Yes, sir. If you will notice the date of the offense—October 31, 1963. It was Halloween night, and I was in college. I was the freshman class president and the student body president and I went out water ballooning. We were egged and drove back to water balloon the guys that egged us and picked the wrong guys. These guys turned us in to the police and we were cited and fined. That was my only encounter with the law, and I have grown up a lot since then. I have no plans to throw anything at anybody ever again. No one was hurt and it didn't cause an accident. But yes, I do have a police record."

The men started laughing. "Son, don't look so serious. We did much worse than that in our college days, but we had the good sense not to get caught. Right, guys?" They all nodded and laughed some more. I think that was their favorite answer.

"Mr. Richmond, let's say you come upon a couple of rough looking college boys that are throwing rocks at the elephants. What do you do?"

"Hmmm. I would ask them politely but firmly not to do it again. If they refused I would notify zoo security. I would think that would be more within their job description than mine."

"You mean to tell me you wouldn't beat the tar out of them?" demanded one of the feisty old men.

"No, sir," I answered calmly. "That would be assault and battery. I can't say I wouldn't feel like doing that, but I'm sure I would leave my family and the zoo open to a lawsuit when the situation could be handled in a better way. The most I would do I think would be to stand between the animal tormentor and the animal. I hope I'll never have to face that problem though. I can see that it could pose some difficult choices."

The men nodded and looked at me in a proud or fatherly sort of way. I felt it was going well but didn't know for sure.

"Last question, son. How do you spend your spare time?"

"Carol and I are very active in our church group. I like to read a lot and study for teaching adult Sunday school."

Dr. Young was one of the interviewers and the director of the zoo. He let out a hearty laugh and said, "Boy, could our zoo stand a Sunday school teacher! I don't know if one of the guys even goes to church, much less teaches Sunday school. I'd be surprised if they did. Yes, we could use a Sunday school teacher for sure." He laughed again and the men joined in the fun. I smiled, not knowing whether or not this was a making or breaking point of the interview. It seemed to have gone well, but I wasn't sure.

"Thank you very much, Mr. Richmond. You'll be notified in two or three weeks as to your status on the list. It was a genuine pleasure talking with you today. Good luck, son."

I left without a clue. Those two weeks seemed an eternity, but time waits for no man. The letter finally arrived. I had moved from forty-two on the list to number two and was later told that my oral exam had been scored near perfect. I had prayed before the exam that God would give me the words to say, and he had. He had also given me the gift of gab in general and I thanked him for answered prayer.

My high position on the list didn't guarantee me anything but an interview. That one was conducted by Dr. Young at the zoo. The first words out of his mouth were, "How's our Sunday school teacher?" Then he turned to the zoo's stone-faced assistant director and said, "This is the lad I was telling you about." The interview went well and ended with the simple statement that I would be notified as to the decision.

I called Dr. Young when I hadn't heard anything after two weeks. He laughed and said, "How's the Sunday school

going!" I said fine and asked him if I was still in the running.
He assured me I was and said they just hadn't gotten around
to making the final decision, but it would be soon.

After two more weeks, I decided it wouldn't hurt to call
again to show my interest in the job. Dr. Young, cordial as
usual, apologized for the delay and said, "Hold the line, son."
I waited on the line for about five minutes. Finally I heard Dr.
Young say, "Mr. Richmond, how about if you give that swimming pool company a couple of weeks notice? We want you
to come work for us out at the L.A. Zoo."

"Thank you, Dr. Young. You just made my day, month,
year! It looks like I'll get a chance at my dream. Thank you
very much."

When I hung up Carol and I celebrated. I couldn't give
notice fast enough. Everybody at the pool company was very
happy for me. And guess what I did for the first year I worked
at the zoo? I took care of their pools in the aquatics section.
Not one person at the zoo knew how to take care of pools
except me. They had become a mess, but with the skills I had
learned from the pool company, we were able to make them
shine like the sun.

The Lord had been my shepherd. He had led me by clear
waters and had shown me how to keep them clear. That
experience and my Sunday school teaching had won the
director over. Against all odds, the Lord proved himself capable of meeting not only my needs but also my wants. I later
discovered that the more educated guys were usually passed
over because they tended not to stay. They looked for hungry
guys that had horse sense, someone who would stick around
and learn the trade.

I left the zoo in 1974 not because I was tired of the animals. That would never happen. I left because I had tired of
the political atmosphere and had lost respect for the current

veterinarians. I told my wife that if someone made me a good offer I would be willing to leave—one of those statements you make, never really thinking it will happen. In a matter of weeks, I was being courted to become the director of a small but pristine little camp in Evergreen, Colorado, which turned out to be another wild story.

God used the seven years to the day that I spent at the zoo! People love animal stories and I have been given many wonderful experiences to share, a great medium for sharing the truth of God. Those were great days. I love my ministry to single parents at the First Evangelical Free Church of Fullerton even more than my time at the L.A. Zoo. But I will forever be thankful to God for the time he allowed me to spend with the fascinating creatures he had made. It was a great ride. Nobody takes care of you like the Lord.

21

Please Don't Feed the Bears

IT WAS LATE IN THE AFTERNOON when we pulled up to the office of Moore's Redwoods—a group of privately owned cabins located in the midst of the most majestic national park in the world, Yosemite. We had needed only to pick up our key to begin our week of vacation.

Leaving our daughters Marci and Wendy in the car, my wife and I were greeted by the manager, a woman in her early sixties. She wore horn-rimmed glasses and welcomed us with a raspy voice, a product of over forty years of smoking. She acquainted us with the campground's rules and shared the ample opportunities for recreation in the area.

A week would never be enough time to see Yosemite's beauty, but we were going to try. As we were leaving the office, the manager added, "Oh by the way, don't feed the bears. We got a big sow and her cubs coming through every night and she's a mean one. Big one too. She's threatened some folks and could be dangerous."

I nodded. I didn't know what Carol was thinking, but I was wondering where one might purchase bear food. I wanted to see this mean old she-bear. Our vacation needed a smudge of adventure to flavor the relaxation.

I wanted to check the Guiness Book of Records to find out

if our six-year-old daughter Marci had asked, "Are we there yet?" more times in a six-hour period than any child before her. I opted for unloading our Buick Estate station wagon instead. During the unloading process, I discovered why they had called it the Estate Wagon. You could haul everything you owned inside and on top of it. It felt more like a move than a trip.

Oh, the sweet relief of carrying the last piece of luggage into the cabin. I flopped down on the couch to rest, closed my eyes, and stretched out. I kicked off my shoes and wiggled into a comfortable position. I took a deep breath, letting the air out slowly as I always do just before I nap.

The stealth bomber prototype then dropped her thirty pound payload to my midsection from the back of the couch and asked if I wanted to play. I have never abused my children, but was tempted at that moment in time. I was falling asleep and thinking about mean bears. Whatever I might have done at that moment would have been in self-defense, but I restrained myself and only went for my daughter's throat for a second.

There are two words whose meaning I could never teach to my children: "Daddy's tired." They always stared blankly, and asked again and again if I wanted to play. I was twenty-seven at the time and still haven't answered the question: "Why did we have children?"

Carol fixed a wonderful dinner that evening, which we ate on the deck in front of the cabin. As it reclined in the west, the sun silhouetted a thousand pine trees. We felt wonderfully revived by the fragrance of pine burning in a dozen fireplaces mixed with the clean mountain air. A family of deer walked through camp and we joined other families in the pleasure of feeding them bread and black oak leaves. A preview of heaven's coming attractions, I thought as I looked at my family and smelled the air. "It doesn't get any better than this."

BEAR BAIT

I was glad we were not able to eat all that Carol had pre-pared. Now we had bear bait. I gathered the bits of corn and salad and placed chicken bones with meat over the top of it all. I carefully placed the food near the bottom of the metal trash can and then put a fifty-pound rock on top of the lid. Around the rock I sprinkled bits of chicken. If this didn't attract the she-bear, nothing would.

We weren't sure when she would come through the camp-ground, but I knew I would hear her if she did. An after-thought insured hearing the bear. I stacked seven aluminum cans in a pyramid on top of the trash can. When the she-bear moved that lid, we would know it. The dishes were cleaned and put away. Then we played Scrabble. Carol won. We had packed some good books, and after putting the girls to bed, we began to read.

At 9:30 p.m. I heard the cans fall. The she-bear was just outside our kitchen window. We turned out the lights in the cabin and Carol and I walked to the kitchen sink. We pulled the curtains apart slowly and peeked through. We were shocked to see the bear only four feet away—standing and massive! This bear had to weigh five hundred pounds, easily the largest black bear I had ever seen.

The night was very foggy and still cold for mid-June. Steam was billowing from her mouth and nostrils in the sixty degree air. The mother bear looked dark and sinister. The cans had apparently frightened her cubs and she was clearly postured to protect them.

We finally saw the cubs trying to pull over the trash can, held fast by a steel frame. The she-bear grabbed the fifty pound rock and pushed it several feet from the garbage can. She deftly pulled off the lid and tried to reach the chicken near the bottom. When that failed she just stuck the top third of her body into the can and stood up again with chicken, corn, and a paper plate in her mouth.

The she-bear finished the food and moaned at her cubs. They quickly snapped to attention and followed her into the foggy night. What a thrill being that close to such an obviously dangerous animal. But that thrill was to pale in comparison with what was to happen the next day.

After a good breakfast we took a drive through the majestic Yosemite Valley. The snow pack in the upper meadows created a massive runoff, and all the falls were thundering. Spray was blowing everywhere. No matter where you look in Yosemite, the effect is absolute awe at God's handiwork.

We examined a display at the ranger station about the destructive power of bears, including examples of bent metal and broken doors—ample evidence for "DON'T FEED THE BEARS." No specific stories were told but it was hinted that many visitors to the park had suffered injuries from bears. Not associating with bears was clearly the best course if you wanted to go home in one piece. The display was sufficient to convince some people to behave responsibly. For a few of us it was simply more fuel for fire. Bears seemed more exciting than ever.

Back at the cabin, we were joined by the Crosleys, close friends from San José, along with their toddler Greg. They planned to spend the next three days with us. Fine times are always best enjoyed with good friends. Knowing Rich was a kindred spirit, I could hardly wait to share the bear adventure with him. Rich was a jet pilot and loved adventure as much as I did.

I was right. Rich was wild about the idea of baiting the she-bear and getting a good look at her. Our barbeque left-overs provided perfect bear bait—steak, beans, bits and pieces of dessert, and salad. Rich and I lovingly collected the garbage and again broke the rules by baiting the garbage can. Our wives protested, saying that these rules had been posted for good reasons. Well, what could you expect? They have both willingly journeyed through adolescence into adulthood. Rich and I had no intention of letting go of childhood.

I tried to explain to our wives that as a junior animal authority, I knew what I was doing. "There are only two rules to stay safe," I proclaimed. "One, don't get between the sow and her cubs. And two, don't get very close to the female." After a little debate Rich and I wore them down.

We played rook, a sort of poor man's bridge, guys against the girls. After two hours we heard the sound of crashing aluminum cans. The she-bear was back.

We turned out all the lights and gathered around the kitchen sink to see her and carefully separated the curtains. There she was! She had already cast aside the large rock and we watched her snap the lid off the can. The bear didn't bother about reaching for the food, but just bent over and began to eat the morsels. We could hear the eerie sound of steak bones cracking like potato chips.

Then the bear stood as she looked around and sniffed at the air. Again billows of steam flowed from her nostrils and mouth. Our hearts all stopped when she turned and looked directly at the window. She was definitely scary-looking. Her brown-stained teeth were visible as she licked the grease from her lips and muzzle. We breathed again when the mother bear looked away, called her cubs, and walked toward the front of the cabin.

"Rich, let's see where she goes from here," I said. He nodded. Much to the frustration of our wives, we stepped out on the front porch. In the glow of the street light, we could see the bear lumbering slowly west. Her massiveness was accented by the smaller cub walking next to her. The bears were draped in fog, an ideal scene for a werewolf or vampire movie.

Now something was wrong with the picture, but we didn't realize right away what it was. From the kitchen window, Carol noticed a lone cub which had doubled back to look for scraps of food. Remembering what I had said about getting between a mother and her cubs, she knew Rich and I were in trouble.

Carol ran to the front door of the cabin to warn us. She grabbed the door handle but the door was stuck. Assuming it was locked, she turned the lock to open it—inadvertently locking it! Not realizing the danger, Rich and I had brazenly walked down the steps to get an even better look at the mother bear.

We suddenly heard one of her cubs cry out behind us, probably frightened by us and asking for help. This bear was a good mother who would allow no possible harm to befall her cubs. She began to charge from about fifty yards away. Her loud roar made it clear that we were in trouble.

Rich was looking at the cub and was just turning to see why the mother roared. I had already started to run for the cabin and ran right into Rich, knocking him flat. I picked him up and shouted "RUN!" His view of the she-bear helped him respond quickly. We were both covering a lot of territory at a cartoon pace. We cleared the six cabin stairs in two strides.

I could hear the bear's breathing and growling just behind. If she caught us, I could picture the headlines:

TWO PRE-ADULTS CAUGHT FEEDING BEAR
BEAR PLEADS JUSTIFIABLE HOMICIDE

I reached the door first, turned the handle, and pushed with all my might. My mistaken impression was that we had been locked out. The reality was that Carol was trying to get the door open from the other side. She was finally able to move it into the unlock position. We pushed the door again and scrambled inside, slamming the door behind us. I threw myself against the door and waited for five hundred pounds of anger to break it down.

Silence, except for the heavy breathing of four terrified adults. Several seconds passed with no bear sounds of any kind. None on the porch and none outside. Our wives—who had run into the bedroom to hide—came out and cautiously peeked through the window. The bears had mercifully left. I sank into a chair and wiped the perspiration off my forehead. We all began to laugh. The nervous laughter soon turned into the boy-was-that-a-stupid-thing-to-do kind.

There is no teacher like experience. I no longer even have to see a sign or be told, "Please don't feed the bears." Close calls don't get any closer than that without becoming a needless tragedy. The memory is funny only because I can laugh at my humanity and am alive to laugh.

One of the signals that I have grown-up is that I now read signs and even consider them. I now understand that they may represent true wisdom instead of someone's attempt to rain on my parade. Rather than obstacles to fun, signs and warnings have become guideposts that will perhaps enable me to live longer and better. I now have a better view of the end of the journey. If I follow the signs, maybe I'll get there in one piece. These days I give my wife less cause to hold her heart and grit her teeth. She takes it as a sign of my love.